SPIRITUAL
HOUSEKEEPING

SPIRITUAL
HOUSEKEEPING

KIMBERLY DANIELS

CHARISMA
HOUSE

Most Charisma House Book Group products are available at special quantity discounts for bulk purchase for sales promotions, premiums, fund-raising, and educational needs. For details, write Charisma House Book Group, 600 Rinehart Road, Lake Mary, Florida 32746, or telephone (407) 333-0600.

Spiritual Housekeeping by Kimberly Daniels
Published by Charisma House
Charisma Media/Charisma House Book Group
600 Rinehart Road
Lake Mary, Florida 32746
www.charismahouse.com

Unless otherwise noted, all Scripture quotations are from the New King James Version of the Bible. Copyright © 1979, 1980, 1982 by Thomas Nelson, Inc., publishers. Used by permission. All rights reserved.

Scripture quotations marked AMP are from the Amplified Bible. Old Testament copyright © 1965, 1987 by the Zondervan Corporation. The Amplified New Testament copyright © 1954, 1958, 1987 by the Lockman Foundation. Used by permission.

Scripture quotations marked KJV are from the King James Version of the Bible.

Cover design by Justin Evans
Design Director: Bill Johnson

Visit the author's website at www.kimberlydaniels.com.

Library of Congress Cataloging-in-Publication Data:
Daniels, Kimberly.
  Spiritual housekeeping / Kimberly Daniels.
      p. cm.
  Includes bibliographical references (p.   ).
  ISBN 978-1-61638-238-4 (trade paper) -- ISBN 978-1-61638-570-5 (e-book) 1. Christian women--Religious life--United States. I. Title.
  BV4527.D29 2011
  248.8'43--dc23
                                      2011021237

11 12 13 14 15 — 9 8 7 6 5 4 3 2
Printed in the United States of America

CONTENTS

Preface: Spiritual Housekeeping   vii

Introduction: As for Me and My House   1

  1   Delivered From Social Intercourse   9

  2   Have No Respect of Curses   21

  3   Understand Realms of Authority   35

  4   Get the Occult Out of Your House   47

  5   Stand for the Truth in Your Home   63

  6   Women on the Wall   71

  7   Woman's *Enemy-Detection* Instincts   81

  8   In the Tent (the Anointing of Jael)   89

  9   Close the Vortexes of Hell to Your Family Bloodline   105

 10   Be Victorious Over Legal Attacks   119

 11   Get the Religious Spirit Out of Your House   139

 12   The Science of God   151

 13   The Apostles of the Science of God   163

 14   Thou Shalt Not Covet   175

 15   The Blessings of Firstfruits   193

Conclusion   217

Appendix: Firstfruit Scriptures   219

Notes   225

Spiritual Housekeeping

I N THE MILITARY, it is important for soldiers to learn, remember, and to activate the general orders of the soldier's creed. As believers, we are soldiers in the army of the Lord! In the pages that follow, by using the general orders of the army as a guideline, I create general orders for you as a watchman of your home.

Watchman of the House General Orders

1. I will be a gatekeeper of everything within the limits of my house and will pay attention to voice of the Lord as to how to deal with the spiritual traffic of my home.

2. I will obey the commandments of the Lord and perform the duties of my calling as a believer and a soldier of the Must High.

3. I will give any sudden terrors, unexpected attacks, and any difficult situations to the Holy Spirit, who is the ruler of my life and the one who covers and protects my home.

He who dwells in the secret place of the Most High shall abide under the shadow of the Almighty.

—PSALM 91:1

As for Me and My House

Has God called you to serve in ministry? Do not take it for granted! Unfortunately, serving in any capacity is taken very lightly in the church. Spiritually speaking, it is one of the most targeted positions in the church. These targets come from different directions and perspectives. First, there are people who want to get close to the man or woman of God for whatever reason. They always make friends with the armor bearer or the pastor's assistant. It amazes me to see people go from being totally unnoticed to being the most popular person in the church simply because of a position. I intentionally choose quiet people who do not have a lot of associations in the ministry to serve as my assistants. They tend to be more focused and have less to distract them.

When we serve in ministry, we are exposed to a lot of sensitive things that affect many lives. I have observed that having too many associations can be a hindrance to service to the Lord. The calling of God puts a demand on our lives to be very selective with our associations. We can never be effective when we are pulled in too

1

many different directions. Also, hanging out with a lot of people can sometimes hinder dedication to confidentiality. When we give people too much access into our lives, it opens doors to breaches of confidentiality. I am not saying that we cannot have friends and associates. I am saying that the more traffic that we allow in our inner circles, the more it opens doors to warfare that we are not called to go through. Priorities and categories are important in relationships. First, we must prioritize our relationships. After trying other ways I have come to the conclusion that the priority order that works for me is God, ministry, family.

I used to think that I was supposed to put my family life before what I was called to do in ministry. I thought this way because everyone else thought this way. It never agreed with my spirit; I just flowed with the status quo. The result was a divorce from my first husband. Whenever you put anything in front of what God has called you to do, it will fail.

Today, my husband and children understand that we are called as a family. They have learned that when we seek the things of the kingdom first, God personally takes care of our family. He would never tell us to neglect our household. God's agreement with me is that if I take care of *His business*, He will take care of *my business*. His business is the ministry, and my business is my family. In the order of God, nothing is left undone. As a matter of fact, I never go on a ministry trip without my house being in order. My husband, the children, the bills, and the things around the house are always in order before I step on a plane. The Lord has given me grace in this area of my life. I travel the world, but my house is in order.

After order is set, there is a flow that will bring the supernatural intervention of the Holy Ghost into my personal and business affairs.

My family understands that sacrifices have to be made for the ministry. We have the mentality and set the atmosphere in our home that promotes the fact that our lives do not belong to us. We know that we have individual callings and understand that we are called as a family. Being in charge of a congregation is a family calling. If everyone in the family does not have the revelation of the calling to be the first family in a church, there will be problems. I thank God that my husband and children love ministry. They are excited about what God is doing through our family and love to travel with me around the world. They know that as a family, WE ARE CALLED TO SERVE!

We are not just a Christian family. We are a family of Levites who abide under the anointing of Zadok. The Zadok anointing refers to Zadok, a high priest in the time of David, who, along with his sons, maintained a standard of integrity and loyalty in their personal lives and taught the people to do the same. In the Bible, the sons of Zadok taught the people the difference between what was holy and was unholy. This anointing must start in the houses of the shepherds of a church. We do not claim to be a perfect family, but we are pressing to represent the Lord as He is perfecting us through His Word daily.

We have made great sacrifices with our finances and our time. At the beginning of our ministry, there were times when we could not go on vacations because of needs in the ministry. In the past we had to put things on hold to purchase things for the church. This has been a witness to my children. Today they see the fruit of the seeds that we have planted as a family. Because of the things we did without, they now experience supernatural provision in their careers, education, health, and all other kinds of benefits that we know came only from God. The favor of God blankets my household, and we know that it has come as a result of serving the Lord as a family.

Because of the service my family has provided to the Lord, I understand my responsibility to serve my husband as a helpmeet. God has called His handmaidens to be helpmeets. The anointing of the helpmeet flows from the woman of the house to the entire family. The man of the house has to be in place to rule as the head

3

of the household, while the helpmeet releases the spirit of servitude in the atmosphere of the house.

The Role of the Helpmeet

I do not believe that men and women can do whatever or be whomever they feel like they can be in the household. I believe that God had established roles in the family. The roles in the family unit make up the organism of the family—which God created. The family is not an institution; it is an organism. It lives because it is filled with lives. The Word of the Lord declares that Jesus came that we might have abundant life (John 10:10). This means that having abundant life in our homes is conditional. Somehow society has gotten off course for what God's original plan was for the family. He meant for marriage to be between one man and one woman. Their union was blessed by God to be fruitful to have children. Because of new customs, new laws, and new ways of thinking, all that God meant for the family to be is at stake. The tolerance of alternative lifestyles in our churches has bred antichrist doctrines that relate to family and marriage. The belief that two men (in a relationship) can raise children is a doctrine of devils. The same goes for two women in a lesbian relationship.

The Bible says because "women exchanged the natural use for what is against nature," and "the men, leaving the natural use of the woman, burned in their lust for one another, men with men committing what is shameful," that "God gave them over to a debased mind" (Rom. 1:26–28). As a result, God Word goes on to say: "Those who practice such things are deserving of death, not only do the same but also approve of those who practice them" (Rom. 1:32).

This debased behavior is definitely acceptable in the world. I have no problem with people doing what they want to do in their homes—this is America. The problem comes in when the beliefs of others with alternate lifestyles attempt to influence what is going on in my household. Two married men or two married women do not fit into the blueprint that God laid out for the family. The man has a role, and the woman has a role—especially when it comes to God's blueprint for parenting. Although God is a father to the fatherless and a mother to the motherless, He determined that the best situation for a child is to have the influence of *both* a man and a woman in his or her life.

I know personally some very nice people who live homosexual lifestyles. I love them, and my heart goes out to them, but I am not God; *He makes the rules!* The rule concerning this matter is clearly laid out in Genesis 1:27: "So God created man in *His own image*; in the image of God He created him; *male* and *female* He created" (emphasis added). God also says that in holy matrimony, "the *two* shall become *one flesh*" (Matt. 19:5, emphasis added). Two men or two women cannot become one. God made a man and a woman like a socket and a plug—they fit together and become one. Power cannot flow through two sockets or two plugs. They cannot become one! Also if two men are together in a relationship (or two women), they do not reflect the image of Christ. A marriage relationship must reflect God's image. Homosexual relationships reflect the image of the antichrist. These words are strong, but true. As believers engaged in spiritual warfare, we cannot bow to the lies of the land. Even the laws that our governments pass and the rules that our churches vote on cannot change the truth in our hearts. We must stand for the truth. When we stand *for truth*, we must *stand against* some things. It is our constitutional right and our faith.

The devil wants to pervert the roles of our families and change the order in our homes. He wants the men to be followers and to be soft, and the women to lead and be hard. There is nothing wrong with women taking leadership in the house. It just becomes a problem when we allow the enemy to pervert the roles. Men can cook and women can bring home provisions, but the order of God must stay intact.

The woman was created *after* the man. God said that it was not good "that man should be alone" (Gen. 2:18). Something was going on in Adam's life before God created Eve that made God notice that something was missing in his life. God did not create another man for Adam; He created a woman. God made Eve to look similar to Adam, but there was something different about her. She was a weaker vessel, but there was an inner strength in her. God made her from Adam's rib so that she could be bone of his bone and flesh of his flesh. She was created to be his helpmeet. The word *helpmeet* is a combination of the Hebrew words *ezer* and *neged*, which mean "help" and "counterpart or mate." It means to render aid, assist or give help. It means to succor, to surround and protect. The word *succor* means:

- "To get beneath"

- "To give assistance in times of want, difficulty or distress"

- "To run to help when in any kind of need"

There are stories that have been passed through folklore about the demon called Lilith and her relationship to Adam. Lilith is a man-hating spirit and cannot stand any submission to men. Lilith is the demonic symbol for the women's feminist movement. The folklore says that Lilith was in the garden with Adam before God created Eve, and this is why God said it was not good for man to be alone. Lilith supposedly wanted to rule over Adam and to even be a dominant control over him to have sex. I cannot confirm all the details of this myth.

But I can confirm that Lilith exists in the Bible. (See Isaiah 34:14.) The Hebrew word *liyliyth* is translated "screech owl" in the King James and "night creature" in the New King James and New International versions. Lilith is a type of *succubus* (demon that manifests as a female to have sex with men). I do know that the succubus demon exists! I have met witches who were women feminists who argued that women were on the earth before men. They hate the authority that God gave to the male seed. Ladies, God has called you to be a *succor* and not a *succubus*. Get under the covering of your husband, and your generations will be blessed. Do not allow the enemy to deceive you into coming into agreement with demon spirits to change the order of God or to pervert the roles He has set in your family.

When the woman takes her place, it really makes it easier for men to get in place. It is like a Rubik's Cube. When everybody gets in place, all the colors line up. When everyone is in line, the greater picture and plan that God has for the family can be seen. When the woman gets in place, if she has a man who fears God, he will be forced to line up. On the other hand, I realize that there are some men who do not fear God. It is very difficult for a woman of God to follow a husband who is following the devil and the ways of the world.

Many women worship Lilith in ignorance by not submitting to their husbands. Some men have male chauvinist spirits and are therefore out of order with God's design. I would be the first to admit that there are serious issues to be considered on both sides of the coin when it comes to marriage. That is why God is so adamantly opposed to believers becoming unequally yoked (2 Cor. 6:14). He hates this more than divorce. There will always be problems in marriages; there are no perfect marriages. But the formula of God for holy matrimony is:

- One man

- One woman

- Being equally yoked

- The constituted order of God in the house

- The ordained roles being in proper place in the relationship

Even after the devil has attacked the order of the house and things are in a mess, it is never too late. I have seen God save marriages that seemed hopeless and over. Only He can make a way when there is no way and work a miracle. I thank God for His mercy and grace flowing through our relationships and our homes! Make it personal and receive it for yourself.

CHAPTER 1

DELIVERED FROM
SOCIAL INTERCOURSE

THE BIBLE TELLS us that believers are "in" the world but not "of" it (John 17:11, 16). God has called us to be a light to the world. At the same time He has warned us not to be unequally yoked with people, places, and things that would hinder our walk with Him. So with this in mind, how do we run our businesses, educate our children, and relate to society in a way that will not displease God or cause us to be unequally yoked with the world? The answer is simple—beware of social intercourse! Let's start by reading 2 Corinthians 6:14–15 (KJV, emphasis added):

> Be ye not unequally yoked together with unbelievers: for what *fellowship* hath righteousness with unrighteousness? and what *communion* hath light with darkness? And what *concord* hath Christ with Belial? or what *part* hath he that believeth with an infidel?

I have read this scripture many times over the past twenty years of my salvation. I found it very interesting that the Holy Spirit would open it up to me in a new way, as He did recently. Though the foundation of my deliverance is rooted in this scripture, until now I never recognized the standard that it sets for a victorious lifestyle in Christ Jesus. Second Corinthians 6:14–15 represents the line that God has drawn in the Spirit to give us:

- Spiritual strength to avoid compromise and ungodly tolerance

- Stamina and endurance against opposition and persecution

- Discernment to know the difference between what is holy and what is unclean

The key words of this passage are:

- *Fellowship*—People (becoming one in Him)

- *Communion*—Places (gathering in His name)

- *Concord*—God (agreement with God)

- *Part*—Faith (having a belief that cannot be shaken)

Fellowship—righteousness vs. unrighteousness

The word *fellowship* is *metochos* (*met'-okh-os*) in the Greek, which means, "intercourse." *Intercourse* is defined as: "connection or dealings between individuals or groups that causes a coupling or uniting that makes those who have come together one." As I studied the word *intercourse*, I noticed the word *interchange*. When intercourse takes place, there is always an interchange. This means that the people who come together literally experience an exchange in the midst of their union. The word *interchange* means, "to put each in the place of the other; to cause to change places, or to give and receive things from each other reciprocally." It also means to cause to follow one another.

Based on the word study on *fellowship*, it is not difficult to see that when we fellowship or socialize with people on a continual basis, a union takes place in the spirit. This is why the Bible asks the question, "Can two walk together, unless they are agreed?" (Amos 3:3).

The interchange involves everyone and enables each person to get something out of the relationship. This is why we must know those that we labor among. God commands that we "come out from among them" (2 Cor. 6:17)! If you do not want what other people have, it would not be wise to hang out with them. On the other hand, when believers come together, there is a sweet communion that takes place. Where two touch and agree, Jesus comes into the midst. One believer can put a thousand demons to flight, but two can put ten thousand to flight (Deut. 32:30).

The Word of the Lord asks: "What fellowship hath righteousness with unrighteousness?" Whenever the Word asks a question, an alarm should go off in our spirits to do a self-evaluation. We should ask ourselves questions like:

- What kind of inner circles am I a part of?

- Are the values of those who are closest to me committed to righteousness or unrighteousness?

- What am I depositing into my closest relationships, and what am I getting out of these relationships that influences me spiritually?

Pause and think on these questions! Is there anything in your life that you are in fellowship with that will stop you from being one with Jesus? If so, break fellowship with it now!

Communion—light vs. darkness

We are called to be in communion with our God. Let's look at the word *communion*. The Greek word for communion is *koinonia*, which means: "partnership, participation, social intercourse, communication and distribution."

I was knocked off of my feet when I found out that communion means *social intercourse*. When Paul refers to communion, he relates it to light and darkness. He is actually saying that light and darkness will never commune or agree. Because of this, we must choose one side with which to commune. There will always be controversy, combat, and a battle in the spirit when dealing with light and darkness. Many people get discouraged when they experience this kind of warfare. This is the kind of warfare we should rejoice about!

The Bible says that we must be watchful when all men speak well of us. The truth of the matter is that not *all men* are supposed to agree with us. All men are not walking in the light of the truth, and when you are confronted with darkness, *there is supposed to be a battle!*

> If the world hates you, you know that it hated Me before it hated you. If you were of the world, the world would love its own. Yet because you are not of the world, but I chose you out of the world, therefore the world hates you. Remember the word that I said to you, "A servant is not greater than his master." If they persecuted Me, they will also persecute you. If they kept My word, they will keep yours also.
>
> —JOHN 15:18–20

The battle will rage when light and darkness collide. The only true light in the world is the light of Jesus Christ. The world hates Jesus! When believers get this down in their spirits, they will develop tougher skin. Those who represent Jesus must have tough skin and not take persecution from the world as a personal attack. It is not personal; it is scriptural! The world is not supposed to love you when you love Jesus. When believers allow resistance and rejection from the world to get them down, it is a sin before God!

Paraphrasing what Jesus said, He made it simple: "Who do you think you are? You are not greater than Me! They hated Me, and I created them—I AM God! Do not be moved when they hate you." This is the commandment of the Lord. Light cannot commune (be comfortable with) darkness. No matter how good things may seem or how nice people may be, if you are a child of light, darkness will always oppose you. No matter how much you try to harmonize, there will be a screeching sound of discord in the spirit. We have Jesus on the inside of us, and demons will always be uncomfortable in His presence. When we step into a place, we bring Jesus with us. There are places where people do not want Jesus around. We should not be alarmed when we are barred and even kicked out of certain places. The power of manifested light in a dark place is a good thing. It reveals to the people that they are in darkness.

It is a glorious thing when the children of God come together to let their light shine. When light connects with more light, the power of God is manifested in the earth realm. The *koinonia* of God flows fluently in the midst of the saints. This is why the anointing of the saints increases with numbers. One can put one thousand to flight, but two...ten thousand! *Koinonia* promotes partnership, communication, and a balanced distribution among the people of God. It is a social intercourse that takes place to give birth to the will of God in the earth realm. Real communion causes God's glory to radiate in the midst of a dark and lost world.

There is something awesome that takes place when God's anointed ones gather. We gain ground in the spirit, and the Lord has free course to move. On the other hand, because of negative agreement there were some places where even Jesus could not heal the sick. When we fellowship with people who are not children of light, we get stuck in a spiritual limbo. To be in limbo means to be *caught between*. Because light and darkness cannot agree, those who try to make them mingle always end up in limbo. The manifestations of limbo are the spirits of struggle, distraction, confusion, and heaviness.

We are *in the world* but not *of the world*. We are commanded to go into the world to be witnesses for Jesus, but the approach and strategy we use means everything. We are called to influence and not to be influenced!

There is a difference between *communion* and *compromise*. Communion brings forth a unity that bonds believers together for God's purpose. When we compromise there is no bonding, but a bowing that takes place. It causes a person to knowingly or subliminally submit to the spirit in charge.

Concord—Christ vs. Belial

The scripture also asks, "What concord hath Christ with Belial?" The word *concord* is *sumphonesis* (*soom-fo'-nay-sis*) in the Greek, and it is defined as: "to be in harmony with, agreement, to stipulate by compact; to concur and support."

Agreement means everything! It affects every area of our lives. We need agreement within ourselves to achieve our everyday goals. Without agreement, our families are dysfunctional and our businesses will fail.

God showed me that agreement is a type of spiritual covering. I believe that this is why Paul used the analogy of Christ and Belial. When we agree with certain things, we come under the covering of a certain ruler. We cannot agree with Christ and Belial at the same time; only one will rule!

Let's take a look at the meaning of Belial:

- A person considered morally worthless

- Good for nothing

- Diseased in the mind

- Hard-hearted

- One who promotes rebellion against God and constituted authority

- Another name for Satan

- Vile, lewd, licentious, corrupt

- That which works against and has no regard for God or the things of God

Understanding the meaning of Belial brings forth a greater understanding of why this spirit has no agreement with Christ. We can be effective in winning the lost in dark places and during dark times as long as we have the revelation that Christ has no agreement with Belial. This is what *accursed* means: "dedicated unto doom or damned by God Himself." If God has killed a thing, we cannot religiously resurrect it. If the root is holy, the fruit will be holy, but if the root is demonically dedicated, the fruit will be cursed.

Christ and Belial simply cannot agree. A biblical meaning for the word *agreement* is, "to marry, betroth or to gather selves until they become one." We cannot attempt to attach Jesus to the accursed thing.

Part—believers vs. infidels

The Word of the Lord asks, "What *part* hath he that believeth with an infidel?" The word *part* in the Greek is *meris (mer-ece')*, and it means, "to share, to be in the same province of or to participate with." It comes from another Greek word, *meros*, which refers to a coast, portion, or to have respect of.

When Paul asked the question, "What part hath he that believeth with an infidel?," it was serious! The word *infidel* refers to one who does not have faith in Jesus Christ as Lord. There is a difference between *believing in Jesus* and *believing that Jesus is the one and only living God*. Few deny that Jesus walked on the earth. Many consider Him a great man or even a powerful prophet. The problem comes in when they deny His lordship! Putting it simple, an infidel is one who denies the lordship of Jesus Christ.

What part does a true believer have with a person who does not believe that Jesus is the Lord and Creator of the universe? None! Believers should have no part in activities that give homage or even respect to other gods. We should not spiritually hang out in territories where demons are attempting to make us bow to the gongs of the land with the intent to overthrow them.

The persecution of Shadrach, Meshach, and Abednego is the perfect example of having no part with infidels. The king made a decree that whenever the gong sounded, everyone had to fall down and give homage to the pagan deity of the land. The Hebrew boys were put in the fiery furnace because they refused to bow. Yeah, I know this is an old Bible story (in the minds of many), but the reality of this story will one day be grafted into the hearts of the saints in America. Many gongs are sounding, and many people who call themselves believers are bowing in our country.

Jesus told Satan, "You have no part with Me" (John 13:8). In this same way we must not be a part of, have a portion with, or participate in modern-day idolatries. There are gongs going off in the spirit bidding Christians in America to bow. These are not ancient gongs as in the times of the Hebrew boys. These are gongs of economic trouble, disasters in the weather, seducing spirits from the rich and the famous, political unrest, peer pressure, idolatrous temptation, and compromise. During times like these we can remain steadfast in the things of God if we focus on our portion. Looking to the left or the right will make us lose the race. We can win if we stay in our lane and allow Jesus to be the author and finisher of our faith. We must be able to stand and declare, "As for me and my house, we will serve the LORD!" (Josh. 24:15). God is using His people to do a great work in the days in which we live, and we cannot come down off the wall.

Let's take a look at how Nehemiah dealt with the temptation to bow to the dictates of the world.

> Then I said to them, "You see the distress that we are in, how Jerusalem lies waste, and its gates are burned with fire. Come and let us build the wall of Jerusalem, that we may no longer be a reproach." And I told them of the hand of my God which had been good upon me, and also of the king's words that he had spoken to me. So they said, "Let us rise up and build." Then they set their hands to this good work. But when Sanballat the Horonite, Tobiah the Ammonite official, and Geshem the Arab heard of it, they laughed at us and despised us, and said, "What is this thing that you are doing? Will you rebel against the king?" So I answered them, and said to them, "The God of heaven Himself will prosper us; therefore we His servants will arise and build, but you have no heritage or right or memorial in Jerusalem."
>
> —NEHEMIAH 2:17–20

The people of God were in a bad situation, yet Nehemiah bragged on His God. His enemies mocked him and called him a rebel, but Nehemiah had a revelation; God was his portion! His source was not in man, so he did not have to bow to them. He also let his enemies know that they had no portion in what God had for him. When we (as believers) know our portion and in whom it is placed, we also know the portion (or legal right) the enemy has to get involved in it—none! The portion of the wicked has no agreement with what God has for us.

The twentieth chapter of Job describes the portion of the wicked. It describes the portion of the wicked to be like a basket filled with curses. It includes the following curses:

- The triumphing of the wicked is short, and the joy of the hypocrite is but for a moment.

- He will perish forever like his own refuse.

- He will fly away like a dream and not be found; he will be chased away like a vision of the night.

- His children will seek the favor of the poor.

- His bones will lie down with him in the dust.

- His food in his stomach turns sour; it becomes cobra venom within him.

- He swallows down riches and vomits them up again.

- He will not see the streams, the rivers flowing with honey and cream.

- From the proceeds of business he will get no enjoyment.

- He knows no quietness in his heart; therefore his well-being will not last.

- In his self-sufficiency he will be in distress; every hand of misery will come against him.

- When he is about to fill his stomach, God will cast on him the fury of His wrath.

- A bronze bow will pierce him through.

- Terrors come upon him.

- An unfanned fire will consume him.

- The heavens will reveal his iniquity, and the earth will rise up against him.

- The increase of his house will depart, and his goods will flow away in the day of His wrath.

The scripture concludes by saying: "This is the portion from God for a wicked man, the heritage appointed to him by God" (Job 20:29). I praise the Lord because we have no portion in wickedness. Today, when the hearts of many are failing them for fear, we must continue to confess Psalm 73:26, which says: "God is the strength of my heart and my portion forever."

We must rebel against or disagree with the things or the ways of the wicked. This is the only way to avoid social intercourse. Social intercourse is the pathway to idolatry, which comes in the name of status quo social activities. God put the need to socialize on the inside of us, but we must do it according to the Word of God. There is a sweet anointing when the brethren dwell in peace under the covering of God's covenant.

We can operate in the midst of those who do not know Jesus, but we must lead and not follow. We must influence and not be influenced. This is the calling we have as the salt of the earth. I call it *blending without bending.*

CHAPTER 2

HAVE NO RESPECT OF CURSES

IN JULY 2009, I started a church in South Florida. It has been very interesting ministering in the midst of so many cultures. I am sure that there are people of many cultures in North Florida (Jacksonville), but they are just not as obvious. With the prevalence of different cultures comes the abundance of idolatry and witchcraft. Under the guise of many other things, witchcraft is literally a lifestyle for many people in South Florida.

Rebellion is compared to the sin of witchcraft, and witchcraft is noted as a work of the flesh in the Bible. (See Galatians 5:19–21, KJV.) Rebellion and flesh are indeed root causes of curses. In this chapter I would like to deal with the root causes of curses and their ultimate source. Understanding the ultimate source of curses promotes a strong foundation for victory in Jesus Christ. I say this because understanding the root source of all curses takes the glory from the devil and promotes the true omnipotence of God. God is omnipotent—He has *all power*! Even the power of the devil comes under the sovereign reign of our Lord Jesus Christ. After defeating darkness and putting it to open shame, Jesus made it clear that *all power* was in His hands. Revelation 1:18 confirms that Jesus has declared that He has the keys (authority over) hell and death.

Spending a lot of time in South Florida has settled a matter in my heart. I am now sure that when it comes to dealing with things in the spirit, a lot of people fear the devil more than they fear God. The ironic thing is that the "fear of God" and a holy lifestyle are the only things that protect a believer from voodoo curses. On one hand, most people are ignorant about voodoo curses. On the other hand, some know too much and fear what they have seen on the dark side. As a result, they give the devil too much attention and credit. I am excited about brothers and sisters who love spiritual warfare, but my warning to them is to always have balance. NEVER highlight what the devil is doing over what God does! The devil loves attention, and he will use manifestations of witchcraft to distract us from the true power of God. Remember, no matter how many demonic manifestations you encounter, the devil's power is limited, and Jesus has *all power*! Matthew 10:27–28 says it best:

> Whatever I tell you in the dark, speak in the light; and what you hear in the ear, preach on the housetops. And do not fear those who kill the body but cannot kill the soul. But rather fear Him who is able to destroy both soul and body in hell.

The truth of the fact is that the devil does not have a heaven or a hell into which to put anyone. He does not run hell—God does! He did not create hell—God did! He is not in charge of hell—in fact, he will be locked up in chains in hell when his time comes! The devil can only do what God allows him to do. He is a deceiver, a liar, and a magnifier of his own power. In actuality, he only has as much power as we give to him. When he was cast out of heaven, he hit the ground mad. He is mad because he knows that his time of exaltation is short. God allowed him to be the god of this world. Even his position over the things of the world is a part of the plan of God to establish His own kingdom in the earth realm. I praise God because the devil is not running anything! He is a condemned being.

We can read Isaiah's account of the devil's future in Isaiah 14:9–20 (AMP):

> Sheol (Hades, the place of the dead) below is stirred up to meet you at your coming [O tyrant Babylonian rulers]; it stirs up the shades of the dead to greet you—even all the chief ones of the earth; it raises from their thrones [in astonishment at your humbled condition] all the kings of the nations. All of them will [tauntingly] say to you, Have you also become weak as we are? Have you become like us? Your pomp and magnificence are brought down to Sheol (the underworld), along with the sound of your harps; the maggots [which prey upon dead bodies] are spread out under you and worms cover you [O Babylonian rulers]. How have you fallen from heaven, O light-bringer and daystar, son of the morning! How you have been cut down to the ground, you who weakened and laid low the nations [O blasphemous, satanic king of Babylon!]
>
> And you said in your heart, I will ascend to heaven; I will exalt my throne above the stars of God; I will sit upon the mount of assembly in the uttermost north. I will ascend above the heights of the clouds; I will make myself like the Most High. Yet you shall be brought down to Sheol (Hades), to the innermost recesses of the pit (the region of the dead). Those who see you will gaze at you and consider you, saying, Is this the man who made the earth tremble, who shook kingdoms?—Who made the world like a wilderness and overthrew its cities, who would not permit his prisoners to return home?
>
> All the kings of the nations, all of them lie sleeping in glorious array, each one in his own sepulcher. But you are cast away from your tomb like a loathed growth or

premature birth or an abominable branch [of the family] and like the raiment of the slain; and you are clothed with the slain, those thrust through with the sword, who go down to the stones of the pit [into which carcasses are thrown], like a dead body trodden underfoot. You shall not be joined with them in burial, because you have destroyed your land and have slain your people. May the descendants of evildoers nevermore be named!

To summarize this passage, the devil is making a whole lot of noise but not saying anything. He makes great men fall, shakes kingdoms, and made the world like a wilderness, but in the end people will see him for who he really is—*a wannabe*. Verse 16 of Isaiah 14 says that kings and great men of the earth will ask: "Is this the man who made the earth tremble?" They will question the validity of his power because he has deceived them with a false power. Remember this: the devil only has the power that God allows him to have for His purpose. The great men of the earth will taunt the devil in hell by telling him, "You are weak just like us! Are you the one that we followed to this dreadful place of eternal damnation?"

The word *weak* in Isaiah 14:10 is the Hebrew word *chalah* (*khä·lä'*), which means: "to be rubbed, worn out, weak, sick, afflicted, stroked in flattery, sorry and wounded." The great men of the earth will realize that the power that the devil had presented to them in the earth was only the spirit of magnification. The devil is a fraudulent being, and his only power is deception. We can really walk in true victory when we focus on the fact that his power is weak and his time is short.

Many believers have a distorted understanding of spiritual warfare. Despite the weakness of the devil's power in comparison to God's, they believe that accepting Jesus into their life automatically wards off all evil. This belief is true, but conditional. The conditions are listed in Deuteronomy 28. In this chapter of the Bible

God tells His people that if they obey His commandments they will be blessed, but if they do not obey His commandments *they will be cursed.* The interesting thing is that there are so many more curses listed than blessings. Why is it significant that God lists more curses? I believe it is because there is a great price to pay when people operate in rebellion against God's Word. Rebellion opens doors in the lives of people and gives demons permission to operate in their lives. Curses are simply manifestations of the operation of demons that have been given access, room, or permission to invade the lives of human beings. This is why Ephesians 4:27 warns us not to give place or opportunity to the devil.

Voodoo in South Florida

Having an understanding of the original source of curses is a remedy to the wrong attitudes about witchcraft. The most important thing that people should know in dealing with witchcraft is not to give it too much respect. I call it *having no respect of curses.* We must walk in the fact that God is the Creator and source of all things. The reverential fear of God gives us power in Him and over darkness. Those who live lifestyles that promote the fear of God do not have to fear curses. Whether a curse comes through generations, incantations, or associations, it can be dealt with by the Word of God. Weapons will always form, but the Lord promises that they will not prosper.

Proverbs 26:2 says that "the curse causeless shall not come" (KJV). The Hebrew word for *causeless* is *chinnam* (khin·näm') and means: "devoid of cost, reason or advantage, free and costs nothing, and is in vain." This actually means that a curse does not come in and of itself. A curse cannot come through a door without a key or authority to be there. The initiation of a curse is not free, because a price has to be paid. This is why Jesus paid the ultimate price. He died on the cross so that we could be delivered from every curse.

As believers we must know and believe this and rightly appropriate it to our lives.

I would like to make a profound statement: "People who do not believe in curses will be the first cursed!" The reason is because the unbelief itself is a form of rebellion. We must ask the question, "What gives any person the right to say curses do not exist, when the Word of God says they do?"

Another observation I have made is that some people believe curses exist, but that they cannot harm them. As a result, despite their belief in the existence of curses, they participate in activities and live lifestyles that the Bible declares will give demons access to their lives. Therefore, the curse has a cause to come!

God says that His people perish for a lack of knowledge. Having *respect of curses* can take place in different ways:

- When people become aware that witchcraft and curses exist but give the issue more credit than it deserves

- When people refuse to admit that witchcraft and curses exist

- When people believe that witchcraft cannot harm them, yet they do things to open doors to it

I agree that some people focus on the demonic too much. On the other hand, to totally ignore darkness is even worse. The key is *balance*. When it comes to dealing in the spirit realm, we cannot ignore spiritual warfare. The balance is that a person should seek to discern or see *in the Spirit* when they see the presence of angels or demons. By learning to really tap into the spirit realm, although "all things work together for good," we will recognize that not all that we see is immediately *good*.

Do Not Be Ignorant of the Devil's Devices

To understand curses, we cannot be ignorant of the devices of the enemy. Second Corinthians 2:11 says that if we are "ignorant of his devices," Satan can "take advantage of us." We *do not* want Satan to *have an advantage over us*. God said that His people are *destroyed* for a lack of *knowledge* (Hos. 4:6). The New Testament gives the specifics of how to gain knowledge in 2 Timothy 2:15, which says: "Study to shew thyself approved unto God, a workman that needeth not to be ashamed, rightly dividing the word of truth" (KJV). Ephesians 6:11 stresses the importance of putting on the whole armor of God so that we are "able to stand against the wiles of the devil."

On one occasion, Jesus warned Peter that "Satan hath desired to have you, that he may sift you as wheat" (Luke 22:31, KJV). He went on to say that He had prayed that Peter's faith would not fail, and told Peter: "When thou art converted, strengthen thy brethren" (Luke 22:23, KJV). Later in his own epistle, Peter teaches: "Be sober, be vigilant; because your adversary the devil walks about like a roaring lion, seeking whom he may devour" (1 Pet. 5:8).

Based on these passages, I feel very safe in saying that the saints of God cannot just take a defensive approach against darkness; we must also take an offensive position. We must DO something. Based on these scriptures, it is not hard to figure out what we must do. We must:

1. *Study* (Greek, *spoudazo*)—To use speed and make effort in being prompt and earnest; to be diligent and give one's best in moving toward endeavors that would cause to learn through labor (2 Tim. 2:15).

2. *Be approved* (Greek, *dokimos*)—Proven, tried, and accepted by God (2 Tim. 2:15).

3. *Have knowledge* (Hebrew, *da'ath*)—Relates to discernment, insight, notion. This word is broken down into three parts: the building of a house by wisdom, the establishment of the house through understanding, and the filling of the rooms of the house through knowledge. This word also describes God's gift through technical knowledge along with wisdom and understanding. Technical knowledge pertains to an art or science of the like; to become skilled or familiar in a practical way or technique through training or study (Hos. 4:6).

4. *Stand* (Greek, *histemi*)—To be in a place of balance, to be established and confirmed, to stand opposing falling; to stand before a judge as the accused; to stand erect as the righteous or upright in the consciousness of acquittal and final approval; to be stationed and endure against the attacks of evil (Eph. 6:11).

5. *Have faith* (Greek, *pistis*)—To have the conviction of the Holy Ghost and belief in the truth of the gospel that causes one to be fully persuaded without any doubt that safe existence will be provided (despite the attacks of the enemy) by God at the end of the present season (Luke 22:32).

6. *Be converted* (Greek, *epistrepho*)—To turn from the things that oppose the ways of God toward God; the breath or spirit of God returning to a dead body; regeneration whereby the principle of spiritual life is imparted to man bringing him under the "dominion of righteousness" and causing a conversion (changing into something different) which is

the human response of faith and repentance coming forth from this new condition (Luke 22:32).

7. *Strengthen* thy brethren (Greek, *sterizo*)—To help your brother to walk in the full strength of God on the inside of him; to make him steadfast in mind and stable in his ways; to confirm and set fast and firm to make settled and secure (Luke 22:32).

8. *Be sober* (Greek, *nepho*)—A state whereby one is not drunk with spiritual intoxication; to be sober and alert in mind as to know what is going on (in the spirit): to be wise and watchful to the point of walking circumspectly, not stumbling and tripping over and into the traps, pitfalls and snares that the enemy has laid out before you (1 Pet. 5:8).

9. *Be vigilant* (Greek, *gregoreo*)—To arise and refrain from sleeping; to be alert and mindful of the threatening dangers with conscious earnestness that will deliver from imminent tests and attacks that God allows to come from the enemy. This word denotes the caution a believer needs to take to avoid anxiety resulting from fear or worry; the general attitude of alertness that believers must have (the duty of vigilance) to be prepared for impending attacks, crisis, trials, or temptations; this state opposes a slack or "sleepy spirit" noted in 1 Corinthians 16:13; Colossians 4:2; 1 Thessalonians 5:6; Revelation 3:2; to be watchful or sober so that one can maintain a sense of calmness or self-control when an emergency arises; to be in a place not to be caught off guard when terror comes by night or arrows hit by day (1 Pet. 5:8).

The definitions above prove that we need to be in a place to understand and do warfare. Let's take a look at what Paul said:

> Do you not know that in a race all the runners compete, but [only] one receives the prize? So run [your race] that you may lay hold [of the prize] and make it yours. Now every athlete who goes into training conducts himself temperately and restricts himself in all things. They do it to win a wreath that will soon wither, but we [do it to receive a crown of eternal blessedness] that cannot wither. Therefore I do not run uncertainly (without definite aim). I do not box like one beating the air and striking without an adversary. But [like a boxer] I buffet my body [handle it roughly, discipline it by hardships] and subdue it, for fear that after proclaiming to others the Gospel and things pertaining to it, I myself should become unfit [not stand the test, be unapproved and rejected as a counterfeit].
>
> —1 Corinthians 9:24–27, amp

To summarize what Paul is saying he made it clear that:

- He was in a competition whereby someone would win and someone would lose.

- His competitor was a specific enemy that he needed to put his finger on.

- He would, of necessity, have to endure hardship.

- He had to be fit to stand the tests of what he was dealing with (trained and educated) so that he would be approved and received by God at the end of the race/battle.

It is also important that we understand the following biblical terms in dealing with spiritual warfare:

1. *Advantage* (Greek, *pleonekteo*)—To have a head start or more than another that is operating from a handicapped position; to take authority over in a position of superiority; to have leverage or the upper hand; to have the ability to defraud or deprive the saints of what is rightfully theirs (2 Cor. 2:11).

2. *Devices* (Greek, *noema*)—The mind of the enemy; his inward reasoning; the way he thinks that causes him to do what he does; his reasoning and discernment; his mental inclinations and prudence; discretion, calculation, judgment, tact, diligence, wisdom (2 Cor. 2:11).

3. *Wiles* (Greek, *methodeia*)—The method or way of the devil to follow an orderly, technical, well-thought-out plan or procedure in doing evil; the art of evil as laid out by the master artist of darkness, Satan (Eph. 6:11).

4. *Destroyed* (Hebrew, *damah*)—To cause to cease and be silent; to make perish unto failure and become undone (Hos. 4:6).

5. *Devour* (Greek, *katapino*)—To swallow whole as in eating or drinking; eaters of blood and drinkers of flesh; from the Greek word *kata*, which means, "to go down from a certain place to a lower state"; the state of Lucifer after the fall (1 Pet. 5:8).

The five definitions above describe what our warfare is all about. It is about Satan's attempt to take advantage of God's people because of the fallen state of their sin nature. Jesus came to destroy the work of the devil. Not understanding this can be a crutch to the believer who is operating from the handicapped position of ignorance.

We must totally lean on Jesus in understanding spiritual warfare. The greater one is on the inside of us. Because of this, we walk by faith and not by sight. The weapons of our warfare are not natural but mighty *through God* to the pulling down of strongholds (that we cannot see). If we fail to receive this revelation, the devil will usurp authority over us and defraud us out of our rightful inheritance of dominion.

As soldiers of the Lord, we are called to study and come against the mind (*noema*) of the devil. He has set up demonic surveillance systems like watchers, scanners, and eavesdroppers to study our ways so that he can lay his snares. The enemy's first place of attack is always the mind. Because we have the mind of Christ, we can take authority over the mind of the enemy. We can bind his traps, snares, tactical plans, and dark ways. We can break the power of and send confusion to the demonic order of his methods so that they will not flow. The devil sends false delusions of failure to shut the mouths of God's elect. Finally, he attempts to swallow the lives of God's people. We must be like fish bones in the throats of our enemies. When the enemy attempts to swallow us, the anointing will irritate his throat (demonic gateways), and he will be forced to spit our prosperity, healing, deliverance, peace, welfare, and joy back up. The gates of hell shall not prevail. Weapons will form, but they will not prosper.

CONCLUSION

After more than twenty years of ministry, I have noticed that curses usually manifest under the following categories:

1. Serious marital problems

2. Chronic sickness and disease

3. Mental or emotional illness

4. Long-lasting financial problems

5. Failure in businesses and careers

6. Generational incarceration

7. Repetitive accidents of all kinds

8. The spirit of death plaguing families, businesses, or churches

9. Nightmares, restlessness, and sleeplessness

10. The inability to maintain positive relationships

11. A wandering spirit that can never be stable or settled (especially in churches)

12. Being stuck in limbo, always *almost* getting breakthroughs that never happen, causing the person to always start over

If you have experienced or are currently experiencing the things I have listed above, pray this prayer aloud:

Father God, in the name of Jesus, I repent of all my sins (known and unknown). I renounce the generational curses of my forefathers and thank You for delivering me from all curses. I believe that a curse cannot come without a cause, and I close every door in my life that has given license to the devil. I confess that darkness has no rule in my life or in the lives of my children. Curses that have come through association are broken. I renounce every ungodly alliance in my life. Curses that have come through incantation are broken. I declare that I am a child of the King, an heir of God, and a joint heir with Christ. Because I am in place and in right standing with God, there is no cause for the demons assigned against me and my family that would allow access to our lives. I renounce the curse of death and destruction, the curse of family disorder, the curse of poverty, the curse of pride, the curse of witchcraft, the curse of whoredom, the curse of perversion, word curses, the curse of religion, the curse of spiritual bondage, and the curse of addiction and habits. Anything that comes to destroy my peace of mind, relationships, resources, financial situation, body, family, marriage, ministry, and my place in God is sent back to the point of its origination.

I bind the threefold cord of the strongmen of destruction, Asmodeus, Abaddon, and Baphomet, up and off of my generations forever, in Jesus's name. I am in right standing with Jesus, and I am living daily to obey His will and His Word. Because of this, the multiple curse spoken of in Jeremiah 16:18 has no cause to come into my life. The curse of idolatry listed in Leviticus 20:1–5 has no cause. The curse of familiar spirits listed in Leviticus 20:6 has no cause. The curse of adultery listed in Leviticus 20:10 has no cause. The curse of incest listed in Leviticus 20:11–12 has no cause. The curse of homosexuality listed in Leviticus 20:13 has no cause.

The Lord destroys the house of the proud, but my family and I will humble ourselves in the sight of the Lord. The curse of the Lord only comes to the house of the wicked. My family lives by faith, for we are the just of the Lord. The house of the wicked shall be overthrown, but I and my house will serve the Lord and prosper. Because I believe on the Lord Jesus Christ, I and my house shall be saved. Amen.

CHAPTER 3

UNDERSTAND REALMS OF AUTHORITY

UNDERSTANDING REALMS OF authority is a safeguard against getting outside of your spiritual coast. Knowing your limitations in the spirit is a must. Understanding realms of authority will also enhance and accent your God-given gifts. It brings correction to our tendencies to rebel. Understanding realms of authority gives us a better foundation in understanding order. It is true, there is no male or female in the spirit—but there is always order. You do not have to worry about proving what you can do when you are subject to God's order. God's order always undergirds true authority, and that which He sets in place cannot be moved.

The authority of God will always be challenged. It is simple; the devil hates believers! Whether it is in the natural or the spirit realm, demonic forces always fight against the constituted authority of God's elect. The words *constituted authority* are very important and must be defined. Constituted authority is that which has been appointed, set up, and established by God. What God has appointed is anointed and cannot be denied.

Many people try to operate in the spirit and do not understand spiritual realms. In order to understand spiritual realms, we must understand realms of authority. Though there are many kinds of authority, spiritual authority is the greatest. If our authority in Christ is by the Spirit, it cannot relate to whether or not a person is a male or female, Jew or Gentile. There is no distinction between them in the spirit.

Some people would give everything they have for religious authority, political authority, or even the authority that comes with fame. Athletes draw from physical authority, while great minds lean on the authority of the intellectual realm. Rich people glean from their financial authority, and the people of the world cannot help but depend on their natural authority. Although spiritual authority is the greatest, it often takes the back burner in the minds of men for the more obvious realms of authority.

Spiritual authority is the secret weapon of creation. Many people in high positions have tapped into this truth. Witches and those from the dark side crave authority in the spirit realm to the point of knowing that authority, when harnessed and pushed in the right direction, can rule over and affect every other realm that exists. By making this point, I must note that there are always opposing authorities in the spirit realm—good vs. evil, dark vs. light, the kingdom of our God vs. the kingdom of darkness. There is a battle going on in the spirit, and it is not a natural one. The real battle is not over land, oil, political positions, or the keys to the stock market. The real battle is over authority in the spirit. Every human being has the potential inside to rule and have dominion in the earth.

In the Garden of Eden, God gave dominion to all mankind, not just to believers. The problem comes into play when believers do not use their access to the spirit realm that God has given them to represent Jesus in the earth realm. The devil has been recruiting men to operate in the spirit realm (on the dark side) since the fall of mankind. The Holy Spirit is wooing us to walk with God again as Adam did in the cool of the day. To be effective in the earth realm, we must do two things:

1. Walk with God in a personal relationship and have nothing before Him in our hearts

2. Walk in the dominion that God has given us in the earth realm

Doing the things I have listed above will confuse darkness. It causes a level of spiritual authority that overrides the authority of those on the dark side. I have an armor bearer who was a crack addict for ten years. He was on crack most of the time while he was in my church. He was also a part of a cult that was involved in the Yorùbá religion form of witchcraft. He was dedicated to the devil and was involved in sacrifices to demons. His wife was studying to become a high priestess in the cult. She was at the church for many years but eventually went back to operating on the dark side. My armor bearer eventually separated from her and was miraculously delivered and is serving the Lord.

He had three children with his ex-wife. After he divorced her, she got into a relationship with another warlock and had two more babies with him. I thought that this young man would never be delivered, but today I witness him living for the Lord wholeheartedly. Recently the warlock that his ex-wife is with flagged him down as he was driving through the neighborhood. My armor bearer was caught off guard, because he knew that this young man was working witchcraft against him. The warlock ran up to him and made amends. He said, "I have fasted seven days for you to die. I have sent spiritual hurricanes and tornadoes to your life, but none of it has affected you." Glory to God! When we walk in power as we walk with God, our spiritual authority overrides all authorities of opposition.

At an early age, I took an interest in mythology. At the time I did not know the Lord and had no interest in reading anything. For some strange reason I became absolutely fascinated with reading stories on mythology. I took classes on the subject in high school and college. After giving my life to the Lord and becoming a deliverance and warfare preacher, I noticed that there was a connection between the spirit realm and mythology.

The importance of what God revealed to me was rooted in the meaning of what a myth actually is. A myth is a legendary narrative that has been verbally passed through generations but cannot be verified. God showed me that just because things cannot be verified does not mean they do not exist. This is why people do not understand how to maneuver in the spirit. Believers are supposed to walk by faith and not by sight. Unfortunately this is not always the case. Second Corinthians teaches that what we see is temporal, but what we cannot see is eternal (2 Cor. 4:18). I am sure most Christians understand what this passage means when they use the word *eternal*, but we need to investigate deeper into the meaning of *temporal*. The Greek word for *temporal* is *proskairos*, and it relates to that which is only for a season and temporarily exists.

The things of the spirit realm are very real, but they cannot be socially, scientifically, or intellectually confirmed. The things of the spirit can only be spiritually discerned. Let's take a look at 1 Corinthians 2:

> But as it is written: "Eye has not seen, nor ear heard, nor have entered into the heart of man the things which God has prepared for those who love Him." But God has revealed them to us through His Spirit. For the Spirit searches all things, yes, the deep things of God. For what man knows the things of a man except the spirit of the man which is in him? Even so no one knows the things of God except the Spirit of God. Now we have received, not the spirit of the world, but the Spirit who is from God, that we might know

the things that have been freely given to us by God. These things we also speak, not in words which man's wisdom teaches but which the Holy Spirit teaches, comparing spiritual things with spiritual. But the natural man does not receive the things of the Spirit of God, for they are foolishness to him; nor can he know them, because they are spiritually discerned. But he who is spiritual judges all things, yet he himself is rightly judged by no one.

—1 CORINTHIANS 2:9–15

This passage of scripture is very clear and to the point. Spiritual things must be spiritually discerned! Intellect, science, or anything that we can relate to in the natural will only distort a clear view of what is going on in the spirit realm. We discern things spiritually by knowing them through our spirit man and not through our natural man. First Corinthians 2:14 says that the natural man cannot relate to the things of the spirit.

How We Relate to Realms

In the remainder of this chapter, in order to help you gain a better understanding of realms, I have listed nine ways that we relate to things.

1. *Spiritually*—how the spirit of man relates to reality and his liberty

We are not supposed to put our hope in the things that we can see because they are temporal. We should focus on what cannot be seen because it is eternal (2 Cor. 4:18). What we cannot see is reality, and man's ability to discern this will determine his state of deliverance versus his state of bondage—which determines his eternal destiny.

2. *Physically*—how the fleshly part of man connects to the world

Man was created from the earth of the ground and filled with the breath of God. He became a living soul. The spirit (breath of

God) of a man gives him the ability to relate to God. Because of the fall of man in the Garden of Eden, his eyes were opened to sin, and he became naked (put on carnality). In essence, the sin nature of humanity was born out of the fall of Adam. When man put on carnality, or his flesh suit, it enabled him to relate (connect) to the world. Since that time men have related to the world or carnal things in this fashion. The flesh connects us to the things of the world and is a barrier that keeps men from properly discerning things of the spirit realm. This is why people fast to kill their flesh so that they can connect to what is going on in the spirit.

3. *Carnally*—how the mind of man relates to the truth

To be carnally minded is death, but to be spiritually minded is life and peace. The carnal mind is an enemy of God because it is not subject to the laws of God, which represent the truth (Rom. 8:6–8). The unadulterated truth confuses intellectually girded men. Because they try to figure everything out by carnal methods and means, something that does not line up with their theories is like foolishness to them. Paul announced that he did not preach the gospel with eloquence of speech. He told the church at Corinth that the message of the cross was sheer absurdity and folly to some. He went on to say: "For it is written, I will baffle and render useless and destroy the learning of the learned and the philosophy of the philosophers and the cleverness of the clever and the discernment of the discerning; I will frustrate and nullify [them] and bring [them] to nothing" (1 Cor. 1:19, AMP). He went on to ask, "Where is the wise man (the philosopher)? Where is the scribe (the scholar)? Where is the investigator (the logician, the debater) of this present time and age?" (v. 20, AMP). He finally notes that the earthly wisdom of the world will fail (v. 21). I love it when he seals the deal by saying that God takes foolish things to confound the wise. Because we live in a fleshy body that caters to carnality, we have to be open to truth, which will take authority over what the flesh and the carnal mind will team up to believe.

4. *Socially*—how man relates to man

God declared that it was not good for man to be alone, so He created a woman for Adam (Gen. 2:18). Since this God-ordained union, man has innately had a need to live and breed in an organized society. The mandate God put on mankind to be fruitful and multiply requires a social structure that meets man's need to socialize according to the order of God (Gen. 1:22). This socialization is rooted in man's need to fellowship with one another under God's covering. When God is not the head of the social structure of man, it becomes socialism, which is the enemy of God. Socialism is an organized structure in society that flirts with communism, until communism finally gets a date. A date with communism always leads to marriage. A marriage to communism mandates a divorce from God, because its underlying agenda is antichrist. The communist system replaces the need of the people for God. Ultimately, *the system* becomes *god*.

5. *Economically*—how man relates to the monetary system and state of his environment

"And Elijah the Tishbite, of the inhabitants of Gilead, said to Ahab, 'As the LORD God of Israel lives, before whom I stand, there shall not be dew nor rain these years, except at my word'" (1 Kings 17:1). God's prophets were very active in economic situations in biblical times, as they should be today. The economy was often affected by judgment that was a result of God's displeasure with man. In Judges 3:12–15, God gave His people over to the evil king Eglon for eighteen years. This king taxed the people harshly, and they began to cry out to God. As God always does, *He raised up a deliverer!* The economic situations of the world can never affect the born-again believer who operates under the covering of the economy of God. As markets flip and flop, and the deception of temporary riches grip the loins of many, stability and faithfulness in the principles of God will keep the righteous.

6. *Financially*—how man relates to the prosperity he is called to walk in as an individual

It is God's will that we prosper as our soul prospers. He does not want us to have worldly gain and lose our lives eternally. Financial and material prosperity was a sign of the provision of God for His people. Ministries are called to walk in financial prosperity as a sign to the enemies of God. In Genesis 26, Isaac walked in so much favor and so many blessings that the Philistines envied him. They put him out of the land, and he prospered even more. Eventually the Philistine king came and begged him to make covenant with them. Isaac questioned the king, "Why do you seek after me when you hate me and asked me to leave your land?" (v. 27). The Philistine king told Isaac that he recognized the favor and blessings of God on his life. God will bless His people financially until the heathens get godly jealousy.

He supplies our needs according to His riches in glory by Christ Jesus, and not according to our natural circumstances and situations or the laws or opinions of man. Many Christians reject the blessings of God because of ignorance or a poverty mentality. The enemy tricks them into believing that money is evil. On the contrary, money answers all things. It is the *love of money* that is the root of all evil.

Everything in God has a balance. As God gives the increase, we are commanded to be good stewards of it by avoiding debt. We are commanded: "Owe no man anything but to love him!" Paul knew how to walk in balance. He knew how to abound and how to be abased. This is the balance of God concerning the matter! (See 3 John 2; Philippians 4:19; Ecclesiastes 10:19; Philippians 4:12; Romans 13:8.)

7. *Politically*—how man relates to his government and how it affects his faith

Proverbs 29:2 teaches that when the righteous are in authority, the people will rejoice. When evil men rule over the people, it will eventually lead to mourning. God commands us to render to Caesar what is his (pay taxes) and submit to those in civil authority who rule over us. These authorities are not supposed to be a terror to law-abiding citizens but to criminals. (See Romans 13:1–6.) On the other hand, the balance is that we must not partake of the king's portion, just as the Hebrew boys refused to do. Their countenances were fairer because they did not participate in the witchcrafts of the land. (See Daniel 1:15; 3:5.) As a result of their obedience, God gave them knowledge, wisdom, and skills that influenced their government. He gave them political positions in an evil regime, which led to promotion. If we continue to be passive concerning laws in the land that affect how we worship, and continue to bow to the gongs of the land, our religious liberties will be taken from us. This has already happened in Canada, England, and in other countries. We are living in a Babylonian-directed age, and we must learn how to be in the world but not of it.

The conviction of the Hebrew boys and their refusal to bow their knees to the system forced the evil king, Nebuchadnezzar, to make this decree: "'Therefore I make a decree that any people, nation, or language which speaks anything amiss against the God of Shadrach, Meshach, and Abednego shall be cut in pieces, and their houses shall be made an ash heap; because there is no other God who can deliver like this.' Then the king promoted Shadrach, Meshach, and Abednego in the province of Babylon" (Dan. 3:29–30). The hearts of evil leaders will not be changed if we do not take a radical position for Jesus! As believers, we must be politically (how we relate to our government) correct. This can only happen through the moral statutes of God.

8. *Morally*—how man relates to the laws of God and responds to what is right or wrong

"If the foundations are destroyed, what can the [unyieldingly] righteous do, or what has He [the Righteous One] wrought or accomplished?" (Ps. 11:3, AMP).

The word *foundation* in this scripture means, "to be politically and morally supported or correct." If the church does not get politically involved and become morally sound, we will continue to experience spiritual degeneration. The ignorance of laws that affect our freedom of religion is the Goliath that is mocking our Christian heritage. Spiritual leaders must come out of the fields where they are battling lions and bears to do battle against this stronghold (giant) of ignorance in the church. It is the responsibility of the priest to teach the people the difference between what is right and what is wrong. The atmosphere of the world demands that all lines be erased, all things be equal, and all gods be categorized under one covering of a mystical higher power. In this atmosphere, there are no rules that support the laws of God, and anything goes. The standard of morality is plummeted to the ground and trampled on by the feet of men who shake their fists at and mock the Most High God.

9. *Worshipfully*—how man is created to worship God

Man was created for one reason only—*to worship God*. We do not survive by bread alone, but by every word that comes out of the mouth of God. This is what true worship is about—renouncing the ways of the world (we were all born in sin) and getting to know God. Getting to know God means to become one with Him. Worship is not just about music, lyrics, or instruments. These are only tools used to worship God. We are called to worship God in spirit and in truth. If the Spirit of the living God is not involved in our worship, and there is no unadulterated truth, it is not *genuine worship*! There are many forms of godliness that perpetrate frauds when it comes to worship. There are also many platforms and venues that are not sanctuaries.

To build sanctuaries unto the Lord, we must first be able to prepare our bodies to be living sanctuaries for the Lord. As we carry the glory of God on the inside of us, platforms and venues of worship will give God the glory that is due to Him. In the day we live in we must be specific. People with great venues are preaching that there are many ways to God. They promote a New Age higher power that deceives people to ignorantly worship the devil. They worship at the altar of the unknown god. We must preach the gospel to people and let them get a revelation that if they are not worshiping Jesus, they are worshiping the devil. Jesus is the Messiah and the Son of the only living God. He is the reason we exist, and it is only in Him that we live, move, and even have our being! This being is rooted in worship. The devil is a fallen foe. He is already defeated, and his only perverted way of getting back at God is to get what God loves most—true worship, in spirit and truth. God is seeking people who will worship Him in spirit and in truth.

Every category or realm of authority listed is needed in the life of the believer. To have spiritually strong houses, we must have the balance to operate in the world while pleasing God at the same time.

CHAPTER 4

GET THE OCCULT OUT
OF YOUR HOUSE

IN THE FALL of 1987, I was a staff sergeant in the United States Army. Around the end of October, I was on my way to Germany to do my second tour overseas. I went to visit a friend whom I grew up with. She was also in the military. She and I were dressing to go out to a party, and she began to sing and dance saying, "One more hour, one more hour!" I asked her what she was talking about, and she said, "It is one more hour to Halloween, my favorite holiday. I hate Christmas!" I looked at the clock; it was 11:00 p.m. on October 30th—one hour before Halloween.

We went to a party, and she got real drunk. I was driving and was not drinking. She picked a fight with a young man in the backseat with her. He started calling her names that men should not call women, and she took one of her four-inch heels and hit the young man in his head. I pulled over and begged for her life. As I looked into this young man's eyes, I realized that I was begging for my life too. He was furious.

We parked in the front of a convenience store, and everyone got out of the car. My friend looked at me and started having flashbacks about when I used to beat her up in school. She started pushing me in my head, yelling, "Hit me now!" Everything was happening so fast it seemed like I was in a nightmare. Something strange was going on, but I could not tell what it was. I had never felt like this in my life. I actually felt as if someone was following me and something was going on that I could not see. I felt like something or someone else was instigating what was going on, but I could not put my finger on it.

My friend eventually became so violent toward me that I had to physically defend myself. When the police arrived, I did not have a mark on me, but she was bloody and bruised. I was an E-6 in the military, and she was a private. I thought, "How am I going to explain this?" I did not know God at the time, but I asked Him if He would get me out of what was going on, I definitely wanted to meet with Him.

I did not have anyone to witness on my behalf of the situation in which I found myself. When the guys who were with us talked with the police, they made it sound as if we were just two street women fighting. I was felt like I was sunk.

By the mercy and supernatural intervention of God, the police let both of us go. The only problem was that my friend and the guys left me, and I did not know how to get home. It was 3:00 a.m. I was in Virginia as a guest of the girl with whom I was fighting. I did not have a clue where I was. To make things worse, the $3,000 the military had given me to move to Germany (for my next duty station) was in my suitcase at the home of the girl I had just beaten up.

I cried all the way to a hotel, where I called Deborah, an old friend whom I knew from the streets in Florida. I knew that she had started going to church, so I figured that she might have some answers. She prayed with me, and I asked a million questions about God. I was really spooked about the Halloween song my friend kept singing. It kept ringing over and over in my head: "One more hour; one more hour!"

After hours of counsel, Deborah said something to me that blew my mind. She said, "The devil is real!" It was like a computer turned on in my head and started booting up. I was not ready for the thought that devils and demons really existed. After being tormented by voices in the crack house and seeing shadows on the streets that I thought were figments of my imagination, I just was not ready for more. But ready or not, the reality of the supernatural hit me in my face. The hardest part to deal with was accepting the fact that if demons were real, they were definitely operating in my life.

God worked out my dilemma in Virginia. I got my money and headed back to Florida so I could catch my flight to Germany. A few years later I accepted Christ in my life, and I never forgot when I officially met the devil in Virginia.

Beware of Debauchery

During my second tour in Germany, my son, Mike, and I were preparing to go trick-or-treating. Halloween seemed to be a big deal overseas. Mike was eight years old, in a new country, and needed some extra activity. He was looking forward to Halloween night. All of a sudden, I started having a very uncomfortable feeling in the pit of my stomach. I began to question Halloween in my mind, but I could not shake how not celebrating it would affect my son. I went into prayer and asked the Lord if I could celebrate Halloween, and if not, why not? I was a brand-new believer, and pleasing the Lord was so serious to me.

I heard the voice of God clearly say, "No, it is debauchery!" I did not know what debauchery was, so I looked it up in the dictionary. I found out that *debauchery* was defined as:

- Corrupt activities of perversion that separated people from their duties to God

- Extreme indulgence in sensual pleasures of uninhibited wild acts that mock God

- Seduction from morality that lowers the standard of living and value of what Christ meant for abundant life to be

- Worldly, physical sensations of revelry and orgies with no moral restraints; these acts erase all lines and limits and are rooted in demonic lust

- Lasciviousness

This was enough for me to cancel Halloween for the rest of my life. My son had a hard time with it, but today he is thirty-one years old, and he eventually got over it. I pray that you will teach your children the way of the Lord no matter how much it hurts their feelings. It is better that their feelings are hurt by the truth than for a lie to hurt their feelings in the long run.

The definitions for debauchery listed above speak loudly to those who have ears to hear. Halloween is definitely not from God and is devilish in nature. It promotes a season of darkness, and it is a celebration of abominations that mock Jesus and what Christianity is really all about. Believers should be led by the Lord in planning evangelistic outreaches to have during this celebration. Outreach can be very effective during Halloween—as long as it is *outreach* and not *in-reach*. In-reach is what happens when the rituals of pagans reach into the church instead of the church reaching out to the world.

Of all of the definitions of debauchery listed earlier, the word *lasciviousness* stood out to me. It is mentioned so many times in the Bible. I did a word study:

1. 2 Corinthians 12:21—Paul said he was fearful that many in the church at Corinth had not repented of the sexual vice, impurity, and sensuality (lasciviousness) they had formerly practiced.

2. Galatians 5:19 (KJV)—This verse lists "lasciviousness" as a work of the flesh.

3. Ephesians 4:19—Paul put pressure on the Ephesians to no longer live as the heathens. He described their perverseness in folly and emptiness of soul. He said that their moral understanding was darkened, and they had alienated and estranged themselves from God because of ignorance and willful blindness. Finally he said that they had recklessly abandoned themselves to unbridled sensuality and they were eager and greedy to indulge in every kind of impurity.

4. 1 Peter 4:3—This scripture speaks of believers who used to walk in lasciviousness, banqueting, abominable idolatries, and revelings. The first question I asked about this passage was: "What is wrong with having a banquet?" This particular word, *banqueting*, is *potos* in the Greek, and it means to have a drinking bout or carousal. The word *carousal* refers to a drunken, noisy feast of revelry. The word *revel* literally means, "hell-raiser or to commit acts that lift up the throne of Lucifer." Rebellion is as the sin of witchcraft, but reveling is an abomination against God that includes acts directly carried out to mock Him. These acts are committed by the godless who shake their fists at God and say, "Satan is lord, where is the God of Israel while we shake

our fists at Him?" The powerful thing about this is that God is not moved or stimulated to respond in man's time. In *His time* the godless will be judged. This judgment will be unto damnation for those who do not repent or have been turned over to a reprobate mind.

5. Jude 4 (AMP)—This scripture needs to be read aloud. Read it with me: "For certain men have crept in stealthily [gaining entrance secretly by a side door]. Their doom was predicted long ago, ungodly (impious, profane) persons who pervert the grace (the spiritual blessing and favor) of our God into lawlessness and wantonness and immorality, and disown and deny our sole Master and Lord, Jesus Christ (the Messiah, the Anointed One)."

Jude begins his letter in the Bible by saying that he is separated and set apart for Jesus Christ. He addresses the readers of his letter by saying that he was impelled and felt it very necessary to make the church aware that certain men had crept into the church of God unnoticed. The King James Version of this scripture says that they turned the grace of God into "lasciviousness." Wow, this is a great gap! The most precious thing a believer can have, the grace of God, has become lasciviousness, which is an abomination before the Lord.

According to Jude, these men hang out unnoticed in the church, yet their fates have already been determined. This means that they have already been turned over to reprobate and depraved minds with seared consciences that can never experience the true grace and mercy of God. The Bible explains that these people nibble at fake grace because they are eternally doomed to never eat the fruit of the real thing. Lasciviousness has its greatest power when it operates through fraudulent men in the church. These men are filled with every kind of demonic assignment to lure and trick those who are far away from God and, as a result, have spiritual doors wide open for such infiltration. We must beware of pseudo-ministers and false angels of light who operate in the church.

Let's take a look at some categories of these people:

- *Pseudologos*—Those who speak a false word (1 Tim. 4:2)

- *Pseudomartyreo*—Those who give a false witness or testimony (Matt. 19:18)

- *Pseudoapostolos*—A false apostle (2 Cor. 11:13)

- *Pseudochristos*—A false Christ (Matt. 24:24)

- *Pseudoprophetes*—A false prophet (Matt. 7:15)

- *Pseudadelphos*—A false brother (2 Cor. 11:26)

- *Pseudodidaskalos*—False teachers (2 Pet. 2:1)

All of these words concerning the *false ones* in the church relate to one Greek word, *pseudomai*, which means: "a lying spirit or that which misrepresents the truth."

Back to Halloween, the Holiday

Now that I have broken down the underlying spiritual atmosphere that Halloween promotes, let's talk about its role as a holiday. The word *holiday* means, "holy day." As we have already studied, there is nothing holy about Halloween. The root word of Halloween is *hallow*, which means, "holy, consecrated, and set apart for service." The name Halloween is a form of mockery against God.

I would also like to pose the question that if Halloween is hallowed, whose service is it set apart for? The answer to that question is very easy—Lucifer! The name Lucifer is a part of the demonic godhead. Remember that everything God has, the devil has a counterfeit. Halloween is a counterfeit holy day that is dedicated to celebrate the demonic trinity of:

- The Luciferian spirit (The false father)

- The Antichrist spirit (The false holy spirit)

- The spirit of Belial (The false son)

The key word in discussing Halloween is *dedication*. It is dedicated unto darkness and is an accursed season with a time-released curse attached to it. A time-released curse is a period that has been set aside and separated to release demonic activity to ensnare souls at a great magnitude. Because Halloween operates under a time-released curse and must be utterly destroyed, it cannot be displaced. In other words, churches must beware of their evangelism during this season. As I mentioned earlier, I can understand providing ministry to children, but we have to be watchful of the time-released curse.

During this period, demons are assigned against those who participate in the rituals and festivities. They are automatically drawn to the fetishes that open doors for them to come into the lives of human beings. For example, most of the candy that is sold in this season has been dedicated and prayed over. Curses are sent through the tricks and treats of the innocent, whether they get the treats from going door to door or by just buying it from the local grocery store. I pray for people who have been delivered from occult activity, and they have confirmed this. Dozens of ex-witches have confided in me concerning this practice. I have also prayed for many witches and warlocks who have shared the fact that they have put razor blades in apples, and other things that I do not feel led to tell in this chapter.

When dedications have been made through time-released curses, the demons cannot tell the difference. Believers must draw lines and be as smart as serpents just as the Bible commands (Matt. 10:16). They should not go into warfare during Halloween with evangelistic outreaches without first counting the cost and understanding what they are dealing with. With the Lord's approval, victory is assured. If church events are initiated out of the realm of the flesh, Hallelujah Night will become Hell Night. The event may go well, but the resultant spiritual residue will be the problem.

Witches and warlocks around the world celebrate the demonic harvest. They always take advantage of the changing of seasons, because they pray to the gods of the elements and seasons. Mother Earth is highly celebrated during the demonic harvest of fall. Witches praise Mother Earth by bringing her fruits, nuts, and herbs. Demons are loosed during these acts of praise. When nice church folks put out their pumpkins on the church lawns, fill their baskets with nuts and herbs, and fire up their bonfires, the demons have no respect for the church grounds. They respect the attention and homage they receive during the season—whether it comes from believers or nonbelievers. Gathering around bonfires is not a secret in pagan worship. As I think back on the bonfires that I attended in my high school during homecoming week (always in the fall), I am amazed at how we ignorantly participated in pagan, occult rituals.

The fire gods of occult worship are:

- *Pyrphoros*—The fire-bearing god

- *Pyripmon*—The fire-breathing god

- *Daidoukos*—The torch-bearing god

- *Phosphorus*—The false light-bearing god

Leviticus 10:10 says it is the responsibility of the priesthood to teach the difference between what is *holy* and what is *common*. Believers are called to do evangelism in the midst of darkness, but they must *know* the difference.

The gods of harvest that the witches worship during their fall festivals are the Corn King and the Harvest Lord. The devil is too stupid to understand that Jesus is the Lord of the harvest 365 days a year. Despite this, we cannot be ignorant of the devices of the enemy. When we pray, we bind the powers of the strongmen that people of the occult worship. The celebration of Halloween is much more than a cute little holiday filled with tricks or treats of fun. It is a time for the gathering of evil that masquerades behind the fictitious characters of Dracula, the Wolfman, mummies, and witches on brooms. These demons that have been presented as scary cartoons are more than someone's figment of the imagination. The acts of decorating a building, dressing up for parties, going door to door for candy, standing around bonfires, and highlighting pumpkin patches can unknowingly entertain a familiar spirit. All of these activities have occult roots. The word *occult* means, "secret." The danger of Halloween is not in the things that are openly promoted to the general public, but in the secret, wicked, cruel activities that go on behind the scenes. While innocent people participate in the public holiday activities that take place, I am sure they would not agree with the hidden practices, which include:

- Having sex with demons

- Orgies between animals and humans

- Animal and human sacrifices

- The sacrificing of babies to shed innocent blood

- Rape and molestation of adults, children, and babies

- Revel nights (raising hell)

- The conjuring up of demons and casting of spells

- The release of time-released curses against the innocent and the ignorant

Biblically speaking, the activities of Halloween can be taken
back to the deeds of the Nicolaitans. In Revelation 2:6, Jesus com-
mended the church for hating the deeds of the Nicolaitans and
stated that He hated them too. What was so significant about the
deeds of the Nicolaitans that caused Jesus to loathe them? The word
hate used in Revelation 2:6 is *miseo* in the Greek, and it means: "to
find utterly repulsive; to abhor; to have a deep-seated animosity
against; to be objectionable and antagonistic against."

It is important to understand that according to church history,
the Nicolaitans were the spiritual descendants of one of the first
deacons, Nicholas of Antioch. (See Acts 6:5.) He is noted as a convert or proselyte, so we can be safe to say that he was converted
from paganism. From the writings of early church leaders, it is
also noted that Nicholas had a ministry of compromise. Nicholas
taught that total separation from occult practices was not necessary.
Nicholas has more than one conversion. First he was converted
from occultism to Judaism. Then he was converted from Judaism to
Christianity. The problem was that he brought things into his con-
versions with him and never totally renounced activities that were
anti-Christian. He was one of the fathers of the lukewarm church.
He taught people to have one foot in the church and the other in
the world. He also caused them to have a high tolerance level for
the occult and paganism.[1] The toleration of paganism, idolatry, and
occultism promotes spiritually perverted environments, which God
hates. He addressed this in Revelation 2:13–16 (KJV):

> I know thy works, and where thou dwellest, even where
> Satan's seat is: and thou holdest fast my name, and hast not

denied my faith, even in those days wherein Antipas was my faithful martyr, who was slain among you, where Satan dwelleth. But I have a few things against thee, because thou hast there them that hold the doctrine of Balaam, who taught Balac to cast a stumblingblock before the children of Israel, to eat things sacrificed unto idols, and to commit fornication. So hast thou also them that hold the doctrine of the Nicolaitanes, which thing I hate. Repent; or else I will come unto thee quickly, and will fight against them with the sword of my mouth.

In this passage, God mentions the seat of Satan. Though there are strategic places that are territorially given to the demonic, the seat of Satan also represents places where satanic activity flows prevalently because atmospheric darkness has been ignited. The word seat is *thronos*, which means: "the power of a potentate; to sit on a throne; a stately seat; a position of high-level demonic authority."

According to the meaning of the seat of Satan in the Greek, it is a place where the atmosphere had been made right to lift up Satan's throne. In Isaiah 6:1, the prophet prophesied that he saw the Lord high and lifted upon His throne, and His train filled the temple. This is the place where the atmosphere had been ultimately ignited to lift up the throne of the Most High. Satan's throne is a counterfeit and can be lifted up only to the bottom of our feet. No matter how much devil worshipers lift up Satan's throne, he and his worshipers are under our feet. Scriptures that support this include:

- Revelation 12:9—Satan, "the great dragon," and his angels were cast out into the earth.

- Luke 10:18—Jesus Himself witnessed the devil fall from heaven like lightning.

- Ephesians 2:6—The believer is seated "in the heavenly places" with Jesus.

- Colossians 1:16—"Thrones, dominions, principalities, and powers" were created for and by God.

- Ephesians 1:19–21—Speaks of the authority of the believer and the exceeding greatness of God's power in us (the same power that raised Christ from the dead). It goes on to say that Jesus is seated in heavenly places "far above all principality, and power, and might, and dominion, and every name that is named." This means that if the name of a strong man was left out—he is a subject to Christ! The good news is that because we are seated in heavenly places with Jesus, the demonic activity that is under His feet is under our feet too!

People who worship the devil make an attempt to lift him up. The truth is, he has already been cast out and down. Many are blinded to this fact, but the day will come when all will know that the devil is already cast down!

Believers must renounce the deeds of the Nicolaitans! The word *Nicolaitan* can be broken down into the compound word, *nikos-laos*. The word *nikos* means, "to conquer," and the word *laos* means "people." (This is where the word *laity* comes from, which refers to the general population of the church.) This is the assignment of the spirit of the Nicolaitans. It targets the innocent and ignorant. God says that His people perish because of ignorance. The spirit that operated behind Nicholas's teachings was assigned to conquer the people. The people were taken captive by a lukewarm false doctrine that made them bow their knees to compromise.

The doctrine of Balaam relates to the witchcraft that the devil continues to use to operate against the church. The good news is that it did not work for Balaam, and it will not work against you.

When we accept Jesus, but refuse to renounce Satan and his practices, we are neither hot nor cold. Jesus hates lukewarmness and declares that He will reject those who are lukewarm and will spit them out of His mouth. The problem with lukewarmness is that it attempts to mix the things of the devil with the things of God. God says that He would rather for us to serve Him or to serve the devil (be hot or cold). "And what accord has Christ with Belial?" (2 Cor. 6:15). As believers, we need to answer that question in our hearts. We must avoid the very appearance of evil. I would not want a demon spirit to mix me up with an occult worshiper.

In 2 Corinthians 4:4 we see that the gods of this age have blinded minds and do not believe. Because of that, they will not allow the light of the gospel of the glory of Christ to shine on them.

But we are *in* the world, not *of* the world. There are two ways to deal with the warfare of living in a society that is under the rule of the god of this world.

1. *Possess the land*—God told Joshua and his camp to go in and "possess" the land, which is *yarash* in the Hebrew. It means, "to go into the land and remove the occupying tenants, and to take their place." This means to displace the ministry of darkness with the ministry of light.

2. *Utterly destroy*—King Saul lost his kingdom because he partook of spoils that God told him to destroy. At the bidding of God, some things must be utterly destroyed. Joshua's camp paid a great price when Achan took the accursed things from the battle of Ai. (See Joshua 7.) A curse came upon the entire camp. God seemed to think that these items were so cursed that He told Joshua to burn Achan, his family, and all of the accursed items. The word *accursed* means "dedicated thing." Concerning the occult, *dedicated* has two meanings: "doomed and dedicated to destruction by God Himself; dedicated

to demons by those have participated in demonic consecrations unto Satan."

There is no doubt in my heart that God is calling us to displace many of the activities of Halloween. One Halloween I spoke at a church that had a "Hell House." When hundreds lined up outside, thinking they were going into a haunted house, they were actually about to be evangelized. Hell House depicted the activities of souls in hell. After the experience, a church setting was made available to lead them to the Lord. Many gave their lives to Christ. This is a modern-day example of possessing the land.

There are activities of Halloween that must be utterly destroyed. Most people have no inclination about the kind of demonic activities associated with this demonic holiday. Many children are kidnapped before the Halloween season to become human sacrifices. The ultimate demonic sacrifice is the shedding of innocent blood. Believers cannot be ignorant of the devices of darkness, and they must be prepared to stand in the gap.

If ignorance has opened doors to time-released curses in your household, *repent*! Declare the Word of the Lord: *"As for me and my house, we will serve the Lord!"*

In closing, my twin boys were born around 9:00 p.m. on October 30. Personally speaking, I did not want to have my babies on Halloween. I am not saying that babies born on Halloween are not blessed. Jesus is ultimately the Lord of every day. Our children are not blessed because of the days on which they are born; they are blessed because they are created by the Most High God!

On October 30 of the year my twins were born, there was great warfare in that hospital. I gave birth to my twins with a lady who was a part of the medical staff leaning over the top of my bed with her head tucked into her arms as she chanted. The doctors in the room acted as if this was normal. My husband and I knew that a conspiracy was taking place. First of all, people do not lay their heads to rest over patients while they are giving birth to babies. Despite the circumstances, my husband and I were not distracted! There were people in that hospital who wanted to get their hands on my twins. Because of ignorance, many babies are secretly dedicated to Satan in hospitals after they are born. Witches work at hospitals too! Just as we have ministers strategically placed in medical centers, angels of light are also on their jobs.

The twins were born, and we never let them out of our sight. I can remember running down the halls of that hospital within a couple of hours after giving birth because doctors were trying to take my children into secluded areas without me. I literally had to get in one doctor's face and say, "Give me my baby!" She kept saying that Elisha (the smaller twin) could not sleep with me because he was not eating enough. I told her that if I could not make him eat, she could not do it either. She shook her head and walked away from me telling her staff, "Give her baby to her!" I walked away pushing my baby down the hall smiling and thinking, "The devil is a liar!"

To put the icing on the cake, I spent Halloween night in the hospital. In the middle of the night, a woman came tiptoeing into my room while the lights were off. She was dressed like a clown and was calling my name in a creepy voice. It was around 3:00 a.m. I sat up in my bed and yelled, "In the name of Jesus, get out my room!" I know that this story sounds made up, but it's really true. I pray that you will take a radical position in keeping darkness out of your house. We really do not war against flesh and blood.

CHAPTER 5

STAND FOR THE TRUTH
IN YOUR HOME

THE BIBLE TELLS us that only one thing will set us free. "And you shall *Know* the *Truth*, and the *Truth* shall *Make* you *Free*" (John 8:32, emphasis added). Notice that I capitalized the words "know," "truth," "make," and "free" in the scripture above. I did this because only the truth that we *know* will make us free! What we refuse to believe or *choose not to know* will put us into bondage. I am convinced that we live in a time when people simply *do not* want to *know* the truth. We must want to know the truth and live according to this knowledge in our homes.

It can be very frustrating to see what is going on in our country and in our churches today, and yet continually speak to deaf ears. America has itching ears, and people are not open to hear words that do not meet their physical needs.

Though there are moves of God in our midst, the spiritual climate in America is cloudy and gray. I plead for those who know the truth and are not afraid to walk in it to be a light in the midst of our spiritually gray situation in America. This must start with our foundation—the family unit.

In 2008, I warned believers of the danger of being needy, dependent, and looking to sources outside of Jesus to supply their needs. I warned them about the judgment on the economy and the price we would pay if we supported unbiblical agendas like abortion and same-sex marriage. The things that I warned of two years ago are happening faster than I could have imagined. What I spoke came to pass as truth, yet many chose to remain blind. They did not want to know the truth!

We are facing perilous times as spoken of in 2 Timothy 3. If we cannot agree that we are in the last days, can we at least agree that times are perilous? The plans of the enemy for America are very clear to me.

- Terrorist prisoners in America already have more rights than American prisoners.

- Today it is estimated that 3,300 babies are aborted daily in our country (50 million since 1973 when *Roe v. Wade* was enacted).[1] The enemy wants to make these numbers phenomenally higher.

- To make euthanasia and mercy killings of the unwanted and unaccepted the norm

- To force churches to hire homosexuals on their staffs under equal opportunity employment laws

- To force preachers to ordain homosexuals

- To force preachers to marry same-sex couples

- To outlaw Romans 1 and, ultimately, the entire Bible, under hate crimes laws

- To label Christians as *haters*, *terrorists*, and *enemies of the state* if they do not submit to things that come against their faith

- To outlaw privacy and monitor the everyday activities of citizens through televisions, computers, phones, and all other communication equipment

- To take over the school system and outlaw home-schools in order to brainwash our children

- To use the media to brainwash the next generation with demonic propaganda

- To use social services to turn children against their parents; any type of physical discipline will be outlawed all together

- To depreciate the value of the dollar so that America will come under one monetary system with other countries of the world

- To break the alliance that America has with Israel

- To take America from socialism to communism to the unlimited control of the beast

These things will happen under the cover of lies. By the time the people realize the truth it will be too late.

When I became a Christian more than twenty years ago, God revealed things to me about computer technology and the spirit realm. I did not write a book or make a ministry out of it. I believe that God just needed for me to *know*. I have not shared this experience many times, but I feel led to share it now. This information is only for those who want to know.

During this experience it appeared as though I was taken up in the heavens. This is the vision I saw:

> I was taken up in the air, and I saw the letters WWJD (which stood for "What Would Jesus Do"). The letters in the name of Jesus seemed to be 3D. I turned my face away from the letters, and the voice of the Lord said, "Look again!" When I turned to look again, I saw the letters WWW, and they began to turn into the numbers 666. I could not tell whether I was in a dream or vision. But I can tell you, *it happened*!

After the vision ended, I discovered the following information during my own research:

1. The Greek word for *image* (image of the beast) in the Book of Revelation is *eikon* (icon). To operate on a computer, we have to click on an icon, which is defined as a symbol or *image* that appears to represent a *command*. The words *image* and *command* are very significant, because this is how the everyday lives of people will be controlled—through the *commands* of the *image* of the beast. The microchip is a very important part in the devil's End Time plan. The only way it can operate is through computer (the beast) technology. Computer technology is advancing so rapidly that we cannot keep up with it. I do not think that people realize how advanced technology will get. It will get *beastly advanced*!

2. Revelation 13:5 says that the beast will be given power to talk. The only way an image can talk is through computer technology.

3. WWW is a symbol for 666.

How do we get 666 from WWW? The Hebrew and Greek alphabets do not have separate characters or alphabets for numbers and letters. Letters are also used as numbers. So each letter is a numerical value. The Hebrew equivalent of our W is the letter *vav* or *waw*. The numerical value of *vav* is 6. So the English WWW transliterated into Hebrew is *vav vav vav*, which numerically is 666.

Special Note: I am in no way saying that we should not use computers. I would not be able to communicate with you without this technology. I am saying that we must be wise as serpents and humble as doves. We cannot be ignorant of the devices of the enemy. We must *know* what time it is! I can assure you that what the devil has meant for evil, God is using for His glory (Gen. 50:20). God is in charge, and even the beast is employed by Him. God is the ultimate authority, and His plan will override all of the devil's plans every time.

Even the name *World Wide Web* should put a check in your spirit. A definition for *web* is: "something that entangles and ensnares; a trap for the innocent and unsuspecting." Though we must use the Internet, we also must know what we are dealing with. I can compare what I am saying to living in Florida. There is a lot of crime on our streets. Because there is crime does not mean I do not go out on the streets. I have to go on the streets to handle my daily affairs; but when I do, I *know* what I am dealing with, and I can watch as well as pray. Take some time to read Revelation 13 for yourself in order to get an understanding of this beast of the End Times. Be prepared by *knowing* what the Bible tells you we will have to deal with in End Times.

Conclusion

Even as I write, things are being put into place to persecute people who know and believe the truth. (This is even happening in America—where we are supposed to have freedom of speech.)

A person in our country who is (nonviolently) radical against issues like abortion and homosexuality will soon be called an *enemy of the state.* My heart skipped a beat when I saw a so-called Christian militia group being arrested by the FBI for plotting to come against the Antichrist.[2] My concern is not as much about this particular militia group as it is about how this situation will be used against other believers who are not part of a violent group. Although this group is in error, and terribly wrong in their approach, the spirit of antichrist is a reality. Will those who believe the Word of the Lord concerning the Book of Revelation soon be compared to radically erroneous people like this?

Let's talk about the hate crimes agenda. It is a perfect example of the scheme of the enemy against believers. I know this may be hard to believe, but soon anyone who will not agree with marrying people of the same sex, ordaining gay preachers, and other activities and agendas that do not line up with our faith will be called a "hater." Anyone who maintains conservative views will be considered a far right extremist. It would be determined that such people would potentially jeopardize the changes that secular humanists have mandated need to occur. Such determinations will be used to undermine the constitution of our country.

I am not a lawyer or a political specialist, but I need to ask this question. Has anyone noticed that we are passing laws in our country that are unconstitutional? Has anyone noticed that our freedom of religion is at risk, because other lifestyles and belief systems are impeding on our faith?

We have a right to believe what God says about homosexuality in the first chapter of Romans. I agree that because this is America, people should be allowed to live gay lifestyles or any other lifestyle that they choose. The problem comes in when I cannot teach my congregation that this lifestyle is an abomination before the Lord—*as my faith teaches*. The truth is that the agenda of the homosexual community in America is more than having the right to be gay; one of its goals is to shut down our right to believe that homosexuality is a sin. The agenda wants everyone to accept the homosexual lifestyle as normal. Advocates do not care that to accept their lifestyle is denial of the faith of many! Muslims get more respect for their faith than Christian citizens of this country.

Years ago the Supreme Court ruled that America was a Christian nation. Christianity was the foundation put in place by our forefathers, and it should be acknowledged today. America is rooted in the principle of freedom of religion, but we cannot forget our roots. Christianity is the root religion of America.

Let's take a look at the abortion issue. How can America agree to the unlimited funding for murdering the unborn that was put in place through the health care bill that was just passed? Who will stand up for the rights of babies who are being mutilated in the name of a woman's right to choose?

The truth is—Jesus is coming back soon! He is coming like a thief in the night. The Word of the Lord is not to be debated. Let anyone who has an ear hear what the Spirit of the Lord is saying to the church. Many Christians are walking too close to the world. They do not look forward to the return of the Messiah. I believe that we should build the kingdom and advance the things of God on earth, but every true believer looks forward to being in *His presence* for eternity.

For those who want to know the truth—there is a clause in the health care bill that goes into effect thirty-six months after it is signed, which relates to microchips being put in babies receiving Medicaid. (Medicaid is not free after all, what a cost!) This is copied from the bill:

(2) CHIP TRANSITION - A child who, as of the day before the first day of Y1, is eligible for child health assistance under title XXI of the Social Security Act (including a child receiving coverage under an arrangement described in section 2101(a)(2) of such Act) is deemed as of such first day to be an Exchange-eligible individual unless the individual is a traditional Medicaid eligible individual as of such day.[3]

I really do not have a problem saying, "God told us so!" America, have we sold our souls for medical benefits? Hmm...microchips? Do I have to say more?

I might as well go further by telling you that we will be soon facing the passing of laws that legalize *forced microchips*. As proof of this statement, consider the example of Virginia delegate Mark L. Cole (R-Fredericksburg), who has sponsored a bill that would protect Virginians from attempts by employers or insurance companies to implant microchips in their bodies against their will. Delegate Cole said that privacy issues are the chief concern behind his attempt to criminalize the involuntary implantation of microchips. He also said, "My understanding—and I am not a theologian—but there's a prophecy in the Bible that says you'll have to receive a mark, or you can neither buy nor sell things in the end times. Some people think these computer chips might be the mark."[4] Other states are working on the same legislation to outlaw forced microchips. The ironic thing is that the same people who are promoting so-called human rights are taking away the greatest rights we have as Americans— our rights to privacy and religious liberty. We need to be hungry for the truth, and bondage will flee from us.

CHAPTER 6

WOMEN ON THE WALL

IF YOU ARE a woman of God, I want to alert you that you are called to be a watcher on the wall, one who stands in the gap to protect your home. The term *on the wall* refers to being a watchman for a walled area. It can be seen in biblical examples of the watchmen who stood on the walls of Jerusalem to keep a watch for approaching enemies. (See 2 Samuel 18:24.)

We have supernatural walls of protection around our homes. These walls are given to us by God to rope off our area of protection. Just because our area is roped off does not mean that the enemy will not try to penetrate it. God calls us to watch as well as pray (Luke 21:36). I have mentioned that the wife is the crown of her husband. She is the radar or the one who surrounds and protects the home with her alertness and prayers. This is similar to the example of a mother lion. The lioness wards off and protects the family of lions from enemy infiltration. We are called to be spiritual lionesses in our homes. To do this, we must understand the anointing of the watchman.

The term *watchman* is mentioned only in the Old Testament, but the watches of the Lord are mentioned in the Old and New Testaments. In the Old Testament there were three watches. In 2 Chronicles 23:6, all the people were instructed to keep the watch of the Lord. In the New Testament, there were four watches mentioned. The example of Jesus walking on the water occurred during the fourth watch. "Now in the fourth watch of the night Jesus went to them, walking on the sea" (Matt. 14:25).

Watches were designated shifts for the people of God to watch for enemy infiltration. Lamentations 2:19 teaches about the first watch:

> Arise, cry out in the night,
> At the beginning of the watches;
> Pour out your heart like water before the face of the Lord.
> Lift your hands toward Him
> For the life of your young children,
> Who faint from hunger at the head of every street.
> —LAMENTATIONS 2:19

Women are called to cry unto the Lord on the behalf of their children and families. The scripture tells us to stay in God's face and to lift our hands toward Him. Staying in God's face represents persistence in prayer, and lifting our hands represents casting our cares on God and giving our problems to Him. There is nothing like the prayers of a wife or mother for her family. God placed a special anointing on women to intercede for their families. He put fire in their mouths to decree the Word of the Lord in the home. When women close their mouths in disobedience to God's mandate on their lives, it is a sin. I believe that this is why the devil is always telling the woman to be silent in the church. A bunch of religious folks got together and misinterpreted the Scriptures to say that women should not be allowed to speak in the church. Unfortunately, this man-made rule was put into force (in the church) to support these erroneous opinions.

Bible history depicts the role of women during the time that Paul wrote the passage for women to be silent in the church. At this time women generally stayed at home while the men attended church. Church was new to everyone, and when the women were allowed to attend, they were often out of order. Men sat in one part of the sanctuary, and women sat in another. If women had questions to ask their husbands, they disrupted the service by yelling across the room. Paul corrected them by telling them not to speak in the church (stop disrupting the service), and to go home and discuss their questions with your husbands.

> For you can all prophesy one by one, that all may learn and all may be encouraged. And the spirits of the prophets are subject to the prophets. For God is not the author of confusion but of peace, as in all the churches of the saints. Let your women keep silent in the churches, for they are not permitted to speak; but they are to be submissive, as the law also says. And if they want to learn something, let them ask their own husbands at home; for it is shameful for women to speak in church.
>
> —1 CORINTHIANS 14:31–35

To have a better understanding of what Paul was really saying, we must look at two things: the meaning of certain words and phrases Paul used, and the culture that they lived in during the time.

The words that we need to pay attention to are:

1. "That all may learn"—The word *learn* is *manthano* in the Greek, and it means, "to learn in any way possible that would cause a person to get a better understanding."

2. "Subject"—This word is *hypotasso* in the Greek, which means, "to be put under authority for the purpose of order."

3. "Confusion"—This word is *akatastasia*, and it refers to "instability, disorder, commotion, and tumult."

4. "Peace"—This word is *eirene* in the Greek, referring to "prosperity, quietness, and rest that sets things at one again."

5. "Silence"—The Greek word is *sigao*, meaning, "to keep close and hold peace."

6. "Obedience"—This word is also *hypotasso*, as shown above for *subject*.

7. "Speak"—The Greek word is *laleo*, meaning, "to preach." *Laleo* is related to another Greek word, *lego*, which means, "to break the silence."

From the study of the meaning of these words, and in keeping with the culture at the time, my interpretation of this portion of scripture would be as follows.

It is important to note that Paul was teaching the people of the congregation on the subject of *order in the church*. The New Testament church had been birthed because the Holy Ghost had penetrated the earth. People were literally filled with the Holy Spirit for the first time and needed to be taught how to flow in the gifts of the Spirit. Teaching order was Paul's first agenda. He dealt with confusion and disorder so that a mockery would not be made out of the things of the Holy Spirit.

He did not just correct the women in the church. Paul wanted absolute submission and order in the congregation. In 1 Corinthians 14:28 he instructed those who had no interpretation of an unknown tongue to be silent. Did Paul mean for all people who did not have an interpretation of tongues to be silent in the church and never to preach the gospel? Absolutely not! The focus of this message to the congregation was not about *gender*; it was about *order*.

The first judge to be called *a prophet* was a woman, Deborah. Surely God would not open Deborah's mouth and shut the mouths of all women in the generations after her. When Paul said, "That all may learn," he wanted the church (in general) to get an understanding of how to flow in the gifts of the Spirit and maintain peace and order in God's house. He addressed the issue of confusion in the church by indicating that it was of the devil. He said that God had not authored or initiated it. In other words, Paul knew that the devil was using unlearned women who had no rule in their spirit to interrupt what God was doing. Of course he said that they could not preach. This limitation was not put on them because they were women, but because they were unlearned and causing confusion. Paul demanded that they stop speaking and be silent.

He was telling the women that they could not speak or preach about what they had not learned. He wanted them to be silent and submit to the order of the service. He said that the women needed to go home and learn from their husbands who had more exposure to how things should flow in church at the time. From that time to this time, women have had plenty of practice in how to carry themselves in church. A majority of churches even today are mainly filled with women. To silence women would be to silence the mouth of the church.

Break the Silence and Wail

The anointing of *lego* has been released in the earth realm. God has broken the silence off of his handmaidens. Whether it is in the pulpit, in the White House, in the marketplace, or in the home, ladies, God has given you a voice to make a difference in your generation. People often focus on what women cannot do. I want to declare that there is nothing that a woman cannot do except to be a man. Ladies, as long as you do not attempt to change who God created you to be, you can *be* and *do* anything.

It is no secret that things happen when *the man with the womb* prays. We give birth to the impossible through intercession. God is calling us to be wailing women who are not afraid to stand in the gap and get on the wall.

In Jeremiah 9:17–22, the prophet spoke to the women of his time. Let's take a look at the Amplified Version of this passage.

> Thus says the Lord of hosts: Consider and call for the mourning women to come; send for the skillful women to come. Let them make haste and raise a wailing over us and for us, that our eyes may run down with tears and our eyelids gush with water. For a sound of wailing is heard [coming] out of Zion: How we are plundered and ruined! We are greatly confounded and utterly put to shame, because we have forsaken the land, because they have cast down our dwellings [our dwellings that have cast us out]. Yet hear the word of the Lord, O you women, and let your ears receive the word of His mouth; teach your daughters a lament, and each one [teach] her neighbor a dirge. For death has come up into our windows; it has entered into our palaces, cutting off the children from outdoors and the young men from the streets. Speak, Thus says the Lord: The dead bodies of men shall fall like dung on the open field and like sheaves [of grain] behind the reaper, and none shall gather them.

It is clear that Jeremiah did not agree with women shutting their mouths. The people of God were under great attack, and he called for the mourning women to intercede. He asked that the women make haste and wail over and for them. He asked them to *speak* the word of the Lord. This means, "to decree, declare, proclaim, and to prophesy." The word *speak* in the Hebrew is *dabar*, and it means to:

- *Subdue*—Jeremiah gave the women authority to deal with their enemies.

- *Appoint*—Jeremiah gave the women permission to set order.

- *Command and bid*—Jeremiah gave the women permission to command.

- *Commune*—Jeremiah gave the women permission to communicate to the people.

- *Destroy*—Jeremiah gave the women orders to abolish and eradicate all antagonistic forces.

- *Give name*—Jeremiah gave women permission to designate and nominate.

- *Promise*—Jeremiah called women to dedication and commitment.

- *Rehearse*—Jeremiah called the women to be perfected through practicing obedience.

- *Be a spokesman*—Jeremiah called for the women to be a voice in Zion.

- *Talk, teach, tell,* and *think*—Jeremiah called for the women to impart knowledge to others through the way that they held conversations, communicated issues, and even guarded their thought lives.

- *Utter well*—Jeremiah called the women to excellence in the articulation, enunciation, and vocalization of the words they spoke.

- *Work*—Jeremiah called for the women to travail and bring forth the will of God through labor.

When Jeremiah commanded the women to speak, he sent them forth in the power of what they were ordained to do. Women are called to take their assignments as spiritual gatekeepers between demonic, spiritual darkness and their families, loved ones, and spheres of influence. In this passage of Scripture, Jeremiah described how spiritual death had entered and what the results had been. He said:

- Death had come through the windows and doors and had cut the children off from outdoors (v. 21).

- Death had also cut off the young men from the streets (v. 21).

Whether it is to intercede for the deprivation of children or for the young men who are chained to the streets, the wailing women of today carry the victory for these captives of sin in their bellies, their spirits. The Hebrew word for *wailing* is *nehiy*, which means, "to cry loud, to lament, to assemble." God has put a war cry on the inside of the woman, and the devil knows it. This is why he does everything that he can to shut her mouth.

Jeremiah also gives reference to "mourning women" (v. 17). *Mourning* is another word for *wailing* and is *quwn* in the Hebrew, which means, "to chant or wail as at a funeral; to lament." When women cry out to God, it gets His attention. When they cry out against the enemy, their cries demand victory! The war cry of the man with the womb is the devil's worst nightmare.

Ladies, as soft and feminine as you are, you are a terror to the devil. The only thing that can change this is if you shut your mouth. You are called to get on the wall and stand in the gap and to open your mouth. In order to do this, you must be vigilant and alert. You cannot sleep through the call to intercession. Isaiah 56:10 says:

His watchmen are blind,
They are all ignorant;
They are all dumb dogs,
They cannot bark;
Sleeping, lying down, loving to slumber.

This scripture refers to dogs that cannot bark. The significance of what God is saying is that dogs are called to bark. A dog that does not bark is not fulfilling its purpose. A dog that cannot alert his master of trouble is a lazy, dumb dog. God put a spiritual bark on the inside of women. We are called to sound the alarm in intercession. This is done on the wall of our homes, our jobs, and our ministries. It is a calling that we cannot sleep through.

We are also called to stand in the gap. Standing in the gap is the greatest level of warfare.

> You have not gone up into the gaps to build a wall for the house of Israel to stand in battle on the day of the LORD.
> —EZEKIEL 13:5

> So I sought for a man among them who would make a wall, and stand in the gap before Me on behalf of the land, that I should not destroy it; but I found no one.
> —EZEKIEL 22:30

Standing in the gap is very important to God. In the Book of Ezekiel, God was looking for a man who would stand in the gap for the land and for the house of Israel. I would like to add that God wants women of warfare to stand in the gap for their homes. The enemy always attempts to take God's people out by attacking the land. When we stand in the gap before God, it is for the land. Ezekiel spoke of the need of "the land" in this passage, just as Jeremiah mentioned how the land had been forsaken. Whenever the land is forsaken, someone needs to stand in the gap before the Lord and intercede on behalf of the land.

To stand in the gap means to get between the devil and what he is trying to do and the purposes of God. This is what it means to make up the hedge. The word *gap* means, "breach or room occupied by the enemy." The word *hedge* means, "wall or enclosure." Based on the meaning of these words, standing in the gap to make up the hedge means:

> To take a strategic position in a designated perimeter to get between the enemy and his plan of attack. It means to be willing to stand in front of the actual fire of the enemy launched, and to be able to quench his fiery darts.

It is impossible to stand in the gap without discernment and the ability to overcome the guerilla warfare tactics of the enemy. We must be able to recognize the enemy and know how he operates. Just as detectives and investigators have profiles of the criminals they are trying to catch, there is a profile of the devil. In the next chapter we will take a closer look at the enemy's profile.

CHAPTER 7

WOMAN'S *ENEMY-DETECTION* INSTINCTS

Thecorrect HE MOST IMPORTANT thing to know in building a defense against the enemy is stated in Ephesians 4:27 (KJV): "Neither give place to the devil." The devil does not need a lot of space in which to operate. The Bible teaches that he needs only a foothold. A slither of a crack or a small point of penetration is all he needs.

The word *devil* is *diabolos* in the Greek. This word can be broken down into two parts: *dia* (which means "entry point") and *ballo*. The devil's name means, "entry point or point of penetration." The devil's main goal is to have a place or position in the life of a believer. The word *place* in the scripture is *topos*, and it relates to an area of operation. The devil needs an area in which to set up his diabolic plans and operations. The greatest challenge in warfare is to keep him from gaining entrance. The enemy gains entrance in our lives when we:

- Refuse to let go of old hurts and wounds

- Do not acknowledge what we have done wrong (confession closes doors to the devil)

- Walk in unforgiveness

- Critically judge others

- Insist on maintaining the right to be right

- Allow the spirit of offense to take root in our hearts

A foundational scripture for the watchman is: "Be sober, be vigilant; because your adversary the devil walks about like a roaring lion, seeking whom he may devour" (1 Pet. 5:8). The word *vigilant* is *gregoreo*, and it means to: "be on guard; pay attention; watch."

The biblical principle of watching voids out the possibility of an enemy or aggressor gaining entrance to our lives. Ephesians 6:11 tells us to put on the whole armor of God so that we may be able to stand against the wiles of the devil. The word *wiles* is *methodeia*. The easy interpretation of this word is, "the methods of the devil," but I would like to break down the meaning of this word even further. When the word *methodeia* is broken down into two parts, it is: *meta* meaning, "with," and *odos*, meaning "road." This means that the plans of the enemy all travel on one road.

The devil has a plan with a destination against each of our lives. He has mapped out our destruction and has a specific way planned to carry it out. He is very strategic and wants to find the fastest, most efficient way to accomplish his mission. Although he is anxious to get the job done, he will wait if he has to. This is why so many people who are godly or in ministry and seem to be doing well find that everything is suddenly crashing around them, often without warning. This is called *sudden terror*. Terrorist attacks are always sudden and unexpected. Terrorists get great joy when their plans catch people off guard. Though the attack is sudden, the plan was not made overnight. The plans of the enemy can be long and drawn out. The devil can be very patient in waiting on the right timing to attack his prey.

Terrorists can plan and train for years for an attack that takes only minutes to accomplish. Just as we have secret agencies that study and are sensitive to the plans of terrorists, God wants us to be prepared for spiritual warfare. We are not to be "ignorant of his devices" (2 Cor. 2:11). The word *devices* in the Greek is *noema*, which means: "the mind of the devil." God does not want us to be ignorant of the *mind* or *schemes* of the devil. It is important that prayer warriors have *spiritual secret intelligence.* How do we get information about the enemy? We get it from the Holy Spirit. He knows all things.

The enemies of the Lord were confused when Elisha was always one step ahead of them in battle. The king was concerned that there was a traitor in their midst. He consulted his experts, and they told him that there was a prophet that saw into his bedchamber (2 Kings 6:11–12). That prophet was Elisha. The Holy Spirit will reveal the secrets plans of our enemies to us—both our natural and our spiritual enemies.

DEVIL, BOO, I SEE YOU!

Nobody can recognize the devil like a woman. God put it on the inside of us. I once had a vision that I was walking around a huge building. Although I was on one side of the building, I could see the devil coming around the corner. Before he turned the corner, I was waiting for him. When he turned the corner, I immediately got in his face and said, "Devil, boo, I see you!"

Since that time, this has been one of my favorite sayings. I even wrote a song called "Devil, Boo, I See You!" The words of the song are:

It's a Holy Ghost, jack devil, we' bringing heat;
All you imps and adversaries, get up under my
    feet…well!
It's by His blood that I have been redeemed;
And nothing by any means shall harm me.
The weapons of our warfare (we're strapped in the Spirit);
Mighty through God, pulling down strongholds.
See, ain't no fear up in here, so make my day…what do
    you want to do with me?
Satan, get behind me.
I resist you, devil—so now flee.
Man don't live by bread alone,
But by every word that comes from the throne.
Strongman…what you all about?
In Jesus' name I cast you out!
I take power and authority over you…
Devil, boo, I see you!

"Devil, Boo, I See You" relates to being ten steps ahead of the devil. This is when the Lord alerts you of trouble before the devil can form his arrows. I was in the military during Operation Desert Storm. When I returned to the United States from real war, I experienced so many miraculous alerts from the Lord concerning dangers that my family faced. Let me share a few of them.

Protected from robbery

One night I was leaving a beauty salon with my children. It was around 11:00 p.m., and we were in a dangerous part of town. As I walked outside of the shop, the Lord spoke to me, "There is a man trying to rob you under that car." I signaled to the children to be quiet and carefully peeped around the other side of the car. To my surprise, a man really was lying under the car on the ground! I screamed, and the salon owner ran the man off the parking lot with a gun.

Protection for a loved one

During this time I was living in an apartment with my youngest sister. She had just graduated from the academy to become a police officer. My sister was very active in the police Olympics, and she went to Miami for a big competition. One night while she was there, I started praying in tongues and could not stop. It was not a convenient time for me to be praying in the Spirit, and it seemed to annoy the people whom I was doing it around. Despite this, I could not quench the unction to pray in tongues aloud. I must have prayed for a couple of hours.

I stopped praying after 11:00 p.m. A little later, my sister called me in tears. She seemed terrorized. After she explained what had taken place, I could understand the terror in her voice. A group of Rastafarians had robbed her and the entire softball team in her hotel. Because they robbed the police, it was no secret that their plans were to kill everyone. The police officers did not have their doors locked, so the robbers barged in and tied up all of the officers.

When it was my sister's turn to be tied up, one of the robbers said, "Man I'm not going to tie her up too tight." Flirting with my sister, he loosened the cord around her wrists and feet. The plan was to tie the officers up in the different hotel rooms and then commence killing them one at a time. When the robbers left my sister's room, she was able to get out of the cords. She quickly used a match to set off the fire alarm. It had to be the Lord prompting her to set off the fire alarm with a match. She does not smoke, so it was even a miracle that she had a match.

The fire alarm went off, the robbers fled, and all of the officers came out unharmed. When my sister shared with me what time it was when this incident took place, I had to lift up my hands to worship the Lord. I was praying in tongues while the devil was trying to murder my little sister. As I was speaking mysteries unto the Lord, I was standing in the gap for my sister's life and soul. She did not know the Lord at this time. The Lord has since confirmed the calling of God on my sister's life with the way He has spared her from so many serious attacks against her life.

Storm protection

About twelve years ago, I was on my way to preach at a small church in Fort Lauderdale, Florida. We were driving in a terrible storm. The rain was hitting the window so hard that I started doing warfare. Though I prayed with understanding, most of my prayer was in tongues. Soon the rain stopped, and we praised God for delivering us from the storm. A few miles away from Fort Lauderdale, I received a phone call that my sister (the same sister that was robbed) had been in a terrible car accident, and they did not know if she was going to make it. She had a small car, and she had been hit by a city bus. Her head was swollen twice its size, and she was not doing well at all. I found out that she was hit by the bus during the same time that I was praying in the storm. God miraculously healed my sister without any long-term injuries. Through this experience, I learned what it really meant to pray by the spirit. My natural understanding was focusing on the storm, but in the Spirit I was standing in the gap for my sister's life. Devil, boo, I see you!

Discernment in a family situation

The Lord has also had me to stand in the gap for my husband. God usually gives me a dream or a vision to warn us about danger. One incident that I will never forget is when He had me warn my husband about a family member. I am sharing this testimony because many people do not know how to do warfare when the enemy is a relative or someone close to the family. Let me warn you; the worst kind of enemy to have is a familiar enemy or a family demon or familiar spirit. People who are part of the family or in relationship with another have easier access to work witchcraft against you. Witchcraft has its greatest power when it comes from within the perimeters of your area of operation or through a close friend. Remember, the devil has to have room (access). It is unfortunate that the enemy can use the people who are the closest to us, but it is true. We pray against demonic soul ties all of the time, but we seem to ignore demonic family ties.

I warned my husband about a particular family member that was close to him. He may have believed me in his heart, but his actions said that he thought I had gone too far. The person that I was warning him about had a son who had spent the night with us. He insisted on taking the boy home, even though I had warned him that the boy's parent was working witchcraft against him. I told him that if he took the boy home, the Lord said for him not to cross the threshold of the door or to go into the garage.

This first confirmation of the word of the Lord was that the little boy fell asleep in my husband's car on the way to his house and had a dream. He abruptly woke up and told my husband that he dreamed that they drove up to his house and a snake was in the driveway. In the dream, my husband stepped out of the car on the snake, and the snake bit him. The little boy said that his parent (my husband's relative) was standing in the driveway laughing when my husband was bitten. By the time the little boy finished telling his dream, they were actually pulling up into his driveway. The relative came out of the house and asked my husband to come into the house to get a package. Remembering my warning, my husband said that he did not have time. The boy's parent then asked my husband to go into the garage to get some luggage. The warning not to cross the threshold or to enter the garage became very real to my husband. He cranked his car and came home.

Later, we had many more confirmations that this person was working witchcraft against my husband, but it all started with this experience.

God is anointing his handmaidens to put their finger on the enemy. No weapons formed against us will prosper, but the faster the weapons are detected, the quicker they will be destroyed.

Ladies, I pray that you will walk in the God-given discernment that you have. Be quickened, be sharp, and do not deny what the Lord reveals. Allow the anointing of Jael to abide in your tent. We will discuss this anointing in the next chapter.

CHAPTER 8

IN THE TENT (THE ANOINTING OF JAEL)

IN THE YEAR 2000, John Eckhardt, my apostolic mentor, prophesied these words to me:

> The anointing of Jael will come upon you!

When these words were spoken, I had never heard of Jael. A lot has happened since that time, and I have done an in-depth study of the story of Jael, a woman in the Bible. Over the years, the Lord has dealt with me about Jael's anointing and the significance of it in the lives of women. Almost ten years after the prophetic word on Jael, I am coming into the knowledge of what God is saying about this particular ministry. I do not consider myself to have *arrived* concerning the subject, but I have paid a price to write of the matter to you in this book.

God has given me an acronym concerning the anointing of Jael:

Jesus's Army (of) Enlisted Ladies

These words have impacted my life to the point that I have incorporated a ministry to women called JAEL. I have started to activate my vision for conferences in cities throughout America called JAEL Conferences. Keeping it real simple, it is a gathering of Jesus's ladies for training in spiritual warfare combat battle. This vision was spoken from the belly of my apostle to my belly, and I have been impregnated with the unction to equip women for battle in their homes. My desire in this chapter is to address ladies who are stay-at-home moms, PTA members, and housewives. Though you are not traveling to the nations or preaching to congregations on a weekly basis, *you are on the front lines!*

The home is the front line of the ministry. Most people think that the home is the rear detachment where ladies hang out while their men go out for real battle. If you believe this, the word of the Lord unto you is that the *real frontline battle* is in the home. If the devil can take us captive in our homes and make our homes strong-holds, he knows we will never get past the front doors of others to win souls for Jesus. The very place that we call *home*—which should be our place of rest and safety—will become a place of bondage if we allow access to the enemy. It is a terrible thing to see signs, wonders, and miracles in places around the world, and then have to go home to lay your head in a place of bondage. Let's take a look at Judges 6:

> And the hand of Midian prevailed against Israel. Because of Midian the Israelites made themselves the dens which are in the mountains and the caves and the strongholds.
> —JUDGES 6:2, AMP

This Scripture passage shows that the enemy (Midianites) launched attacks against the children of Israel that caused them to build themselves into strongholds. The use of the word *den* is very significant. The word *den* usually refers to a place where a person resides or lives. The children of Israel built themselves strongholds to dwell in that were located in their own homes. This is the greatest level of bondage a man (or woman) can have—*to be bound in your own home!*

Ladies, before we can win the world, *our homes must be won first!* I am not saying that we will not have children who are in rebellion against God or husbands who do not serve the Lord. I am saying that when we (Jesus's Army of Enlisted Ladies) get in place, the devil is a defeated foe. Though men are the heads of the house, ladies, you are the gatekeeper. Remember, you are the crown that God speaks of in Proverbs 12:4. It means that you are virtuous and war worthy. If you are not enlisted in the army of the Lord, my prayer is that you will be by the end of this chapter. Strap up your boots, gird up your loins, and put on the whole armor of God. The Lord is about to equip and anoint you to beat the devil down in your own house. Not only is He about to equip you to deal with the personal attacks against your household, but He is also about to stir you up and ignite you concerning the call of God on your life. You can cook dinner, keep the house, homeschool your children, be the love of your man's life, and fulfill the high calling of God without ever leaving your house. Biblically, this is called being a *woman of the tent.*

> Most blessed among women is Jael,
> The wife of Heber the Kenite;
> Blessed is she among women in tents.
>
> —JUDGES 5:24

THE STORY OF JAEL

It is erroneous to believe that the only way that women can be on the front lines of ministry is to preach in pulpits, feed the homeless, have television shows, or to write Christian books. All of this is great, but frontline ministry is not limited to these things. Another important way is when the anointing of Jael comes into play.

In Judges 5:24, Deborah spoke a blessing over Jael and called her a woman of the tent. Deborah also said that Jael would be blessed above all women of the tent. This blessing came upon Jael because God used her as an apostolic pioneer to exhibit how we can destroy the enemy in our very own homes. The word *tent* is *'ohel* in the Hebrew language, and means: "tabernacle; dwelling place; covering; tent; home."

In biblical times, people lived mostly in tents. Jael was a housewife, and she was married to a man named Heber. Heber was a Kenite, which was of the children of Hobab, the father-in-law of Moses. Heber had broken all ties with his people and was a friend and had made peace with Jabin, Sisera's king. Sisera was the commander for the army that was coming against God's people.

Barak was the commander for the people of God. He insisted that he would not go to battle against Jabin and Sisera unless Deborah went with him. Deborah agreed and prophesied that Israel would win the battle, but a woman would get the credit (Judg. 4:8–9). By first glance at the story, it would be easily assumed that Deborah would be the woman who would get the credit. She was on the front lines. She judged Israel and was a fivefold ministry prophetess. She is the one whom the commander of the army refused to go to battle without. But I love how God takes the foolish things to confound the wise and the weak things to conquer nations.

Deborah was a true woman of authority. Women of true authority know how to delegate authority. They know how to release ministries that they will never get the credit for. Deborah understood the principle that one plants, another waters, but only God can bring the increase. God used her to pass the baton in the Spirit to her spiritual sister, Jael. She prophesied a word from the Lord that ruled over Jael's head until the enemies of God were defeated.

Barak and Deborah sang about the demise of Sisera with these words:

> They fought from the heavens;
> The stars from their courses fought against Sisera.
>
> —JUDGES 5:20

Deborah's words held so much prophetic power that they released the angels against Sisera. He was already defeated before the battle started, because it was not being fought by power and might. The reinforcements of the Lord were also waiting to assist Jael in taking out this great enemy of the people of God. I did a word study on the word *stars* in the scripture above, which means angels. The stars were aligned over Sisera and Jael, and destiny had already taken its course. Sisera was a defeated foe, and Jael was the victor.

Deborah commanded Barak to rise up because God would deliver Sisera into his hands on that day. The precision of her prophetic word did not give room for thought. The moment of victory had arrived. Everyone had to get in place to receive it:

- Deborah had to speak the word.

- Barak had to obey the word.

- The angels had to line up in the heavens.

- Jael had to be in place in her home.

- Sisera had to die.

The story of how Jael gained the victory over Sisera shows her willingness to do whatever God told her to do to protect her home and her nation. When Barak and the army of Israel overcome Sisera and his army and defeated them, killing every soldier, Sisera fled away on foot and landed in the tent of Jael. She fed him, assured him he had nothing to fear, and waited until he fell asleep. Then she took a tent peg and a hammer in her hand, and "drove the peg into his temple...so he died" (Judges 4:17–23).

There are so many variables in spiritual warfare. So many things are working together for our good behind the scenes so that God will ultimately get the glory. Jael was just a simple housewife in the eyes of many, but there was something very special about the position she held in her house. Though she honored her husband as the head of the household, *she did not deny her calling as the gatekeeper!* She knew that her husband was at peace with things that did not please God, but she held her position. A wife cannot change the heart of her unsaved husband, but because she is sanctified, God will give him grace for a while.

> For the unbelieving husband is sanctified by the wife, and the unbelieving wife is sanctified by the husband; otherwise your children would be unclean, but now they are holy.
> —1 CORINTHIANS 7:14

Though we believe God to the end for our marriages, this teaching even says that there is a time to let them go. Though Jael did not have to let her husband *go*, she did have to come out of agreement with his alliances. Submission is a hot topic in marriage, and it ought to be. Some wives are not submitting to godly men that they should be submitting to, and some are submitting to ungodly men that they should have let go according to 1 Corinthians 7:14. God hates divorce, but the first principle to marriage is that He hates when we are unequally yoked. The key is lining up. Everyone needs to line up with the Word and the will of God. But as we can see with Jael's story, even when this is not the case, God will have mercy on your house.

THE STORY OF
NABAL AND ABIGAIL

Let's take a look at the story of Nabal and Abigail. Nabal was the head of his house, but he did not rule in wisdom. Despite this fact, God had mercy on his household through the wisdom of his wife, Abigail. Abigail was a woman of good understanding; however, the Bible says that Nabal was churlish and an evildoer (1 Sam. 25:3, KJV). The definition of *churlish* is, "to be stiff-necked, stubborn, severely cruel; hard-hearted and in trouble with God." I hear many messages on women who act as Jezebels in marriages. These messages are definitely needed, but where are the messages on Nabal? The spirit of Nabal represents the man who is not a good steward of his constituted authority as the head of his household. Yes, he is the head of the household, but his evil demeanor and the way he handles things causes him to end up the tail. Notice that the Bible also says that Nabal was an evil man (v. 26), and a son of Belial (v. 17).

This means that he is in direct opposition to the things of God and refuses to take heed to His voice. The pride of Nabal was bringing destruction to all of his generations. David was about to destroy him and his entire household. Abigail told David that Nabal was a man of folly (v. 25). In other words he was a foolish man. To be foolish means to have no wisdom. Wisdom is that which leads to victory, but folly or foolishness leads to defeat. Nabal's decision to reject David's request for provision for his army was a foolish one and brought the possibility of destruction and defeat upon his house. Abigail's defiance to her husband and her good understanding and wisdom in the situation removed the possibility of defeat from her house. Her wisdom brought her victory. Abigail made haste when she heard about her husband's foolish decision on the behalf of her family:

- She went to meet David (v. 20).

- She repented on the behalf of her household (v. 28).

- She gave David the provision he requested (v. 27).

Abigail humbled herself before David and confessed that her husband was an evil, foolish man. She stated that he was as his name suggested—*foolish*. She begged David to spare her family and not avenge himself. She reminded David that he was a good man and that he should not shed blood causeless. She asked David to let the Lord deal with him. One sure sign of a foolish man is the fact that he does not leave room in his decision-making process for the Lord to deal with him. David was a man of wisdom, and he heeded the wisdom of Abigail. He said that her advice was blessed because she had stopped him from shedding innocent blood and taking his own matters in his hands. (See 1 Samuel 25:23–33.)

Abigail's wisdom saved her family. She was not on the front lines of battle with David, but her influence brought victory to her house. She was a woman of the tent. When Abigail returned to Nabal to give him the good news, it was as bad news to him; his heart died within him, and he became paralyzed (v. 37). Ten days after that, the Lord smote him and he died. David heard of Nabal's death and returned to take Abigail as his wife. I really do not know why people are so interested in soap operas and reality shows—the stories in the Bible get as real as you can get!

BACK TO JAEL

The story of Nabal is an extreme example of a man being out of the will of God in the house, but it is real. Of course, as women of the tent, we always believe for our spouses to the end. We just cannot ignore the story of Nabal and the fact that God put it in the Bible for us to learn from it. Men can learn how to avoid becoming like Nabal. Women can learn to be in place whether you are married to a Heber or a Nabal. For you ladies who are married to Prince Charming, you can move on to the next chapter.

There are other women reading this chapter who are living in a stronghold in their own homes. I prophesy that there is deliverance for you and your husband (no matter how far he is away from God). Nabal is the spirit of the foolish, evil man, and Heber is the spirit of the passive, lukewarm compromising man. Just remember that these are *spirits* and not men. Come against these spirits, and command the devil to let your husband go!

When Jael killed the enemy in her house, it affected an entire nation. You can pray over and use the principles that Jael used to destroy the enemy in her house to affect your life, your home, your neighborhood, your church, your city, your state, and your nation.

The strategy of Jael

1. Jael went out to meet Sisera (a type of enemy). She was not in denial. She confronted the problem in her house and faced it head-on. She did not wait for the enemy to come into her house. She went out to him and invited him in (Judg. 4:18). We cannot be afraid to invite situations in that we do not want to deal with. Sometimes we have to allow things to manifest or come out of hiding (in our homes) so that we can kill them at the root.

2. She covered Sisera with a mantle (Judg. 4:18). The word *mantle* comes from the Hebrew word *camak*, which means, "to take hold of in a favorable or unfavorable sense." Though she put matters in the hands of God, Jael took control of the situation.

3. When Sisera asked her for water, she gave him milk (Judg. 4:19). The word *water* (*mayim*) relates to filth,

and the word *milk* (*chalab*) relates to purity in this particular scripture. When we face the attacks of the enemy in our homes, it is important that we do not get pulled into filth. The devil loves to makes us think that we have a right to do wrong. Wrong will always be wrong, and right will always be right. Wrong promotes sin, and right promotes holiness. When the enemy tries to tempt us to give him what he wants (filth), we must give him holiness. Beginning with our thoughts, coming through our words, and ending up in our actions, we must purpose not to give the devil what he wants.

4. Jael destroyed Sisera with a tent peg and a hammer (Judg. 4:21). As Sisera slept, she drove the peg through his temples. She used what was in her house to kill the thing that had come against her family. Notice that Jael put the peg in Sisera's head. We are told in 2 Corinthians 2:11 not to be "ignorant of the devices" (*noema* in the Greek) of the devil. This word relates to another Greek word, *noeo*, which means mind. God does not want us to be ignorant of the *mind of the devil* and how he does things. When Jael put the peg in Sisera's head, she destroyed the plans of the enemy against her house, and it ultimately brought deliverance to her nation. Sisera was a strong man who fought against Israel. All the armies of the Lord could not take him out, but God used a woman of the tent to finalize his demise.

5. Sisera asked Jael to stand in the door and say that he was not there (Judg. 4:20). Ladies, to get ultimate deliverance from a situation and to eventually

take control over the enemy, *you may have to tell it!* This too must be done in wisdom and by the leading of the Holy Spirit. That which you refuse to tell when the Lord has commanded you to tell is a demonic secret. Demonic secrets harbor strong forces of darkness. The devil loves to hold things over our heads and keep us captive in our minds. I realize that everything cannot be told all of the time, but there are some things that must be spoken in due season. The devil is defeated by the blood of the Lamb and the word of our testimony. When Barak showed up, the prophecy was fulfilled! Sisera was delivered into the hands of Barak because of a woman…but not just any woman, *a woman of the tent!* And she was not afraid to tell it.

Confession of the Proverbs 31 Woman

Use these confessions in your prayer time to decree and declare the virtues of the Proverbs 31 woman over your life. Read the points aloud and then pray them prophetically as the Holy Spirit gives you utterance.

- I will open my mouth to speak on the behalf of those who are left desolate and defenseless. I will be a voice for the innocent unborn babies who are murdered continually in my city.

- I will open my mouth to judge righteously and administer justice to the poor and needy. I will open my hand to the poor and fill the hands of the needy, whether they are needs of mind, body, or spirit.

- The virtue that God has given me makes me capable and intellectually equipped to do whatever He has called me to do.

- A lack of discernment will cause me to be overlooked. Who can find me? Those who look will discover that my value is precious and outweighs the value of silver and gold.

- My husband (or husband-to-be) confidently trusts in me in his heart and relies on me in strong security. Because of this he has no lack in honest gain and no need of dishonest spoils.

- I am anointed to comfort, encourage, and do good to my husband as long as there is life within me.

- I seek out wool and flax (skills that I use in my home that bring great income to my family), and I work with willing hands to develop it.

- I am like a merchant ship that brings food to my home from afar.

- I rise in the night to get spiritual food for my household. I give a portion of this to my maids, and they are endowed with spirituality to accomplish the tasks to meet the needs of my home. Anyone who aids, serves, or assists me in my house will be blessed. Out of faithful servitude, they will receive great reward.

- I have great business sense. I consider fields and buy them. Though I am a woman of the tent, the marketplace anointing is on my life. The anointing to occupy and merchandise will cause me to plant fruitful vines in my vineyard. My fruit will remain and not fall to the ground. My businesses will prosper! They will work for me, and I will not be overwhelmed by working for them.

- I am girded with spiritual, mental, and physical strength. I am healthy, my mind is clear, and I will walk with God in the cool of the day. My arms are strengthened to carry the load of my days. I can do many things at one time and excel in all of them.

- I have the ability to taste and see that the labor of my hands is good. I have good endurance, and my lamp will burn continually. I will not be overwhelmed and burned out.

- I will not fear the snow for my family. I have worked hard during the months with good weather. My family has sustenance saved for hard times, and they are doubly clothed with scarlet.

- I will make for myself coverlets, rugs of tapestry, and cushions. Creativity is in my loins. I have garments of the priesthood in my wardrobe. The clothes that I wear are of the best material. God has taught me quality over quantity. I make fine linen garments and lead others to buy them. I set the trends and styles in my city. Even the heathen woman wants to look like me.

- My husband is well known in the gate of my city. He sits among the elders of the land, and his counsel is sought after around the world. He does not walk in the counsel of the ungodly, stand in the way of sinners, or sit in the seat of the scornful. Other men seek his counsel because they desire what he has in his marriage. My husband is fulfilled spiritually, emotionally, and physically through my relationship with him. There are no doors open in his life to cause him to give ungodly counsel.

- I am clothed with strength and dignity, and my position is strong and secure. I am secure and confident in who I am, and my husband does not have any hang-ups about it.

- I rejoice over my future. Great things are ahead for my personal endeavors, my marriage, my children, and even my extended family. Every omen or demonic prognostication against my future is overturned by my rejoicing in the great things that God is about to do.

- My mouth is opened in skillful and godly wisdom. The law of kindness is on my tongue to give godly counsel and instruction.

- I look well to how things go on in my house. The bread of idleness, discontent, and self-pity I will not eat.

- My children will rise up and *call me blessed!* My husband will boast and praise me, saying, "Many daughters have done virtuous and noble things, but my wife excels them all. She is a woman of virtue and excellence!"

- Charm and grace are deceptive, and beauty is vain because it is temporary. This is why I will be a woman who reverently and worshipfully fears the Lord. Because of this I will be praised.

- I will be given the fruit of my hands. I am a hard-working woman, but my labor will not be in vain. My rest is in the Lord, and my own work will praise me in the gates of my city. Amen.

There may be things in this confession that you are far away from in your marriage. Despite this, confess each one with boldness! Speak things that are not as though they were—*and soon they will become a reality!* Whose report will you believe for your household?

CHAPTER 9

CLOSE THE VORTEXES OF HELL
TO YOUR FAMILY BLOODLINE

M ANY PEOPLE DO not want to talk about hell. The thought that it really exists is something they discount and cast away as foolishness. Not only should we acknowledge that hell exists, but we should also make sure all members of our households *miss hell and hit heaven like a bull's-eye*. I do not know about you, but "as for me and my house, we *will serve the* LORD" (Josh. 24:15, emphasis added).

The prophet Isaiah gave the following prophetic woes in relation to hell:

- "Woe to those who rise early in the morning, that they may follow intoxicating drink; who continue until night, till wine inflames them!" (Isa. 5:11).

- "Woe to those who call evil good, and good evil; who put darkness for light, and light for darkness;

who put bitter for sweet, and sweet for bitter!" (Isa. 5:20).

- "Woe to those who are wise in their own eyes, and prudent in their own sight!" (Isa. 5:21).

- "Woe to men...who justify the wicked for a bribe, and take away justice from the righteous man!" (Isa. 5:22–23).

Isaiah says that because of these sins, hell enlarges itself and opens its mouth beyond measure. (See Isaiah 5:14.) He goes on to say that "as the fire devours the stubble, and the flame consumes the chaff, so their will be as rottenness, and their blossom will ascend like dust; because they have rejected the law of the LORD of hosts, and despised the word of the Holy One of Israel" (v. 24).

The definition of the word *woe* is: "a state of physical and mental suffering, affliction, agony, anguish, distress, hurt, misery, pain, torment and wretchedness." It also means, "to be put in the place of a fool." Only a fool ignores the woes of God.

God revealed to me that when people willfully continue to disobey the woes (or warnings) of God, angels are released to execute the judgment of God. After studying the Scriptures, I feel safe in listing what I call the Angels of Woes:

- The Angel of Fear

- The Angel of Pain

- The Angel of Pestilence

- The Angel of Famine

- The Angel of Destruction

- The Angel of Death

- The Angel of Horror

- The Angel of Terror

God uses angels to carry out His vengeance against those who dare to defy Him. Angels work for God at His bidding, and when they are released, it is not always good news. Disobedience to the woes of God releases the judgment of God. Judgment is a bad word in the world today. Few acknowledge the judgments of the Lord. They do not pay attention to the fact that God created heaven and hell. People (even preachers) make excuses about the judgments that God releases to get our attention. This chapter is filled with scriptures to support the fact that God is a God of love—but at the same time a God of vengeance. He literally takes it personally when He says that vengeance belongs to Him. Micah 6:9–16 (AMP, emphasis added) warns us to "Hear the rod!"

> The voice of the Lord calls to the city [Jerusalem]—and it is sound wisdom to hear and fear Your name—*Hear (heed) the rod and Him Who has appointed it.* Are there not still treasures gained by wickedness in the house of the wicked, and a scant measure [a false measure for grain] that is abominable and accursed? Can I be pure [Myself, and acquit the man] with wicked scales and with a bag of deceitful weights? For [the city's] rich men are full of violence; her inhabitants have spoken lies and their tongues are deceitful in their mouths. Therefore I have also smitten you with a deadly wound and made you sick, laying you desolate, waste, and deserted because of your sins. You shall eat but not be satisfied, and your emptiness and hunger shall remain in you; you shall carry away [goods and those you love] but fail to save them, and those you do deliver I will give to the sword. You shall sow but not reap; you shall tread olives but not anoint yourselves with oil, and [you shall extract juice from] the grapes but not drink the wine. For the statutes of [idolatrous] Omri you have kept, and all

the works of the house of [wicked] Ahab, and you walk in
their counsels. Therefore I will make you a desolation and
an astonishment and your [city's] inhabitants a hissing, and
you shall bear the reproach and scorn of My people.

There are two important understandings of the word *rod* in this
passage. First, a rod (*matteh*) is an instrument of chastisement, and
looks like a branch taken from a tree to punish. This rod can be
for chastising and correction, and is referred to as a supply of life.
We are warned by God that there will be repercussions if we fail
to correct our children. The Bible goes as far to say that if we beat
our children with the rod, they shall not die (but live). The power
of the rod delivers their soul from hell (Prov. 23:13–14, KJV). Laws
are becoming more stringent in America concerning the physical
discipline of our children. These laws take away our rights to discipline our children when they are young and in our homes, and
gives these rights to the prison guards to beat them in the prisons
when they become adults.

The word *rod* also means, "scepter of authority." So when we
ignore or do not reverence the rod of God, we disrespect His
authority. God commands His people not to ignore, but to pay
attention to His chastisement, correction, and the instruments that
He chooses to *give life*! God warns us that if He does not get our
attention, we will die. He declares that He will not count us as
pure and acquit us when we are as guilty as the wicked. This is
why God commands us to be holy. "Come out from among them"
(2 Cor. 6:17) is the Word of the Lord for the times in which we live.

The curses mentioned in Micah 6 (AMP) that were released as a
result of God's judgment of Jerusalem are:

1. They received deadly wounds that made people sick
   (v. 13).

2. People were laid desolate, to waste and deserted because of their sins (v. 13).

3. They ate food but were never satisfied; emptiness and hunger remained in them (v. 14).

4. They carried away goods and those they loved but failed to save them (v. 14).

5. Those who God allowed them to deliver would be given to the sword (v. 14).

6. They sowed but did not reap (v. 15).

7. They tread upon olives but could not be anointed with oil (v. 15).

8. They extracted juice from grapes but did not drink the wine (15).

9. They were bound by the generational curses of Omri and Ahab and walked in their counsel. Because of this, they were made desolate, and the people of the city released a sound of scorn (hissing) against them. They were ridiculed, mocked, rejected, refused, ignored, and treated with contempt (v. 16).

Have you ever heard messages that teach that God does not cause sickness? The scripture given in Micah 6:13 confirms that this statement is wrong. Not only does God cause sickness, but He also releases poverty (they sowed but did not reap), famine, desolation, and hopelessness. Exodus 34:7 says that generational curses may even be a result of God's wrath upon the guilty.

In a nutshell they faced the judgment of God, a bad word in most church settings. Notice that in this particular passage, God's judgment is not against heathens. God's wrath was against His people in Jerusalem. Most people deny that God causes things to happen through judgment, because they do not have a revelation of hell. *America needs a divine revelation of hell!* Though many preachers want to avoid the topic, having a revelation of hell will give the saints hope in the difficult times in which we live. A revelation of hell will heal the depressed saint quickly. Understanding what the Bible says about eternal damnation will make you see that *things are not that bad after all; in fact, they can be worse.*

There will be no rescue teams or relief efforts in hell. As bad as the current problems of economic downturn, joblessness, terrorism, rampant crime, extreme weather conditions, and escalating perversion may seem, *it could be worse.*

The strongman of hell is hopelessness! This is the ultimate destiny of those who make decisions in life without including Jesus Christ. The devil has set social and political traps to ensnare even the minds of people who attend church against the truth. Through politics, religion, and entertainment, he spews the venom of humanistic teachings to promote the agendas of hell. Abominations like homosexuality and abortion are vehicles to first-class tickets to hell. The ideologies that support such things are manifestations of Baal worship and idolatry. In the name of human rights, they are creating sinkholes for souls to sink into and thereby be damned forever in hell.

Hell is enlarging its borders. A month ago during my prayer and study time, God dealt with me about earthquakes and tsunamis. My intercessory class was given the assignment to pray over and research the topic. Through this research, I was made aware of the domino effects that are happening due to earthquakes that are registering over 5.0 on the Richter scale every day. The day before a major earthquake took place in Chile, Japan had a 7.0 magnitude earthquake. Earthquakes have been happening throughout history—but there is a major difference. In the decade of 1990 to 2000, only about 7,000 deaths were reported from the largest and deadliest earthquakes each year, but in the decade of 2000 to 2010, a whopping 318,000 deaths have been recorded.[1] *Hell enlarged itself* for every soul who died in these earthquakes without knowing Jesus Christ as his or her Lord and Savior.

Matthew 24:7 mentions "earthquakes in various places." There is great controversy over the interpretation of this passage. Some believe that this speaks of what happened in biblical times; others say this passage refers to what is happening in the days we live in now. I believe that both views are correct, but the important thing to note is that earthquakes do relate to the signs of the times.

I also believe that the earthquakes that are happening around the world are a result of hell being enlarged. I realize that this may be too deep for some reading this book to swallow, but give me a chance to explain. Most people are bound by what they can see and have no discernment of what they cannot see. If you have an ear to hear what the Spirit is saying to the church, what I am saying will not be hard to receive.

Isaiah 14:9 (KJV) says, "Hell from *beneath* is *moved* for thee to meet thee at thy coming: it *stirreth* up the dead for thee" (emphasis added). The words I emphasized in that verse are very important:

1. "Beneath" is *tachath* and indicates the lowest part of hell.

2. "Moved" is *ragaz*, indicating to quake, quiver, violent emotion, shake, tremble, and trouble.

3. "Stirreth" is `*uwr*, which means to wake up and open the eyes.

This scripture shows us that hell has something to do with the moving or quaking of the earth. Early in my salvation, God revealed to me that fault lines are vortexes to and connected to hell. Matthew 16:18 declares that "the gates [*pyle*] of hell" (KJV) shall not prevail against the church. The actual meaning of *gates* is, "entrances, gateways, or openings by which to travel." I believe that demons travel to and from hell as they are released to do the devil's bidding. The thing I like about revelation is that though it cannot be proven to be right (because it has been revealed by God), it also cannot be proven to be wrong. Just remember that *revealed truth must be spiritually discerned.* The carnal mind cannot discern things of the spirit!

Most Christians believe that the devil exists and there is a hell. False doctrines are being taught (in some churches) that say there is no hell and the devil does not really exist. Those who teach this are teaching *doctrines of devils.* They tend to sway as far away from the judgment of God as they possibly can.

God is the Creator, and He rules over and judges all that He has created. Not only does God execute judgment—*but He is the judge!* Hell was created as the ultimate proof of God's judgment of those who go against Him and His plan for their lives. It is as simple as this: When we disobey God's Word, we come against Him. Heaven and earth will pass away, but not God's Word. That which has been released out of the mouth of God will not return unto Him void. God promises to punish those who disobey Him. Judgments are released into the earth so that men and nations will repent and be in right standing with God. Judgment is not a bad thing for those who are in right standing with the Master.

The spiritual climate in America waxed cold when the focus in life was geared toward morality without spirituality. We began to focus on what *man could do* and not on *what God could do.* Without spirituality it is impossible for a man to be moral. Morals count, but they must fall under the covering of spirituality. Morality without spirituality is dangerous, because what is considered moral can change with time.

It is sad to say that the change that has come to America has put in a stronghold of the *broad and wide view.* The broad and wide view has shifted morals to the point that people are killing babies like throwing away unwanted chicken eggs. The foundation of the traditional family has been put in jeopardy as women marry women and have babies through scientific methods. The younger generation is being brainwashed with a distorted view of the family unit. I believe that people should have the right to choose their lifestyle, because God gave each person a will. But the problem arises when society begins to force the *broad and wide* lifestyle on people who choose to maintain traditional family values and tries to enforce this view on the institution of the church. Under this campaign of change, the government, media, Hollywood, and other popular platforms are dictating values that clearly undermine our faith and label us as haters if we do not agree.

While America frantically fights for more rights and benefits, the last earthquake caused the earth's core to shift. I do not expect the world to know what time it is, but where are the prophets and intercessors in the church? The Bible is manifesting itself before our very eyes. Biblical prophecy is coming to pass before our very eyes.

Isaiah 14 goes on to say that hell is waking up, "even all the chief ones of the earth" (KJV). It indicates that great men of the nations will be in hell asking Satan: "Have you also become as weak as we? Have you become like us? Your pomp is brought down to Sheol, and the sound of your stringed instruments; the maggot is spread under you, and worms cover you. How you are fallen from heaven, O Lucifer, son of the morning!" (vv. 10–12). Verse 15 of the same passage continues by saying: "You shall be brought down to Sheol, to the lowest depths of the Pit."

So many people willingly worship the devil for fame, fortune, and power. On the other hand, many are worshiping at the altars of unknown gods as they did in the Book of Acts. Under the guise of careers, riches, and popular habits, idolatry is at an all-time high in America. A simple definition of an *idol* is, "a person, place or thing with a demon attached to it that draws people to worship."

Idols take a person's time, money, and attention—*all things that God requires that we give to Him.* There is no latitude for giving any of these things to other gods. God does not want us to put other gods before Him. These gods will eventually push God out.

There are too many references to hell in the Bible; only a fool would say that it does not exist! A person who does not believe in hell does not believe in the Bible, which is blasphemy against the Holy Scriptures.

The names of hell in the Bible are:

- *Sheol*—The place of the dead; called the grave or the pit (Isa. 14:15)

- *Hades*—The place of departed souls (Luke 16:23)

- *Gehenna*—The place of everlasting punishment (Matt. 5:22, KJV: the Greek meaning of "hell" in this verse is *geena*, meaning "Gehenna")

- *Tartaros*—The deepest abyss of Hades (2 Pet. 2:4, KJV: the Greek meaning of "hell" in this verse is *tartaroo*, meaning "Tartaros")

In Job 26:5–6, we discover that "dead things are formed from under the waters, and the inhabitants thereof." It says that "hell is naked" and "destruction hath no covering" (KJV). The Hebrew word for *destruction* is *'abaddown*, which means, "the abode of the dead."

When we combine that meaning with Revelation 9:11–12, we learn that the name of the angel of the bottomless pit is *Abaddon* in Hebrew, thereby identifying Abaddon as the demon of destruction. The verse also tells us that his name in Greek is *Apollyon.*

After verse 11 refers to the bottomless pit, verse 12 follows by saying: "One woe is past. Behold, still two more woes are coming after these things." It is important to review the "woes" or "warnings" of God mentioned in the Bible when we are trying to understand the judgment of God. Every time you see the word *woe*, it is like a spiritual stop sign—we must stop and not continue in the direction of the things that God is warning us about.

This reminds me of the Old Testament depiction of Balaam and his donkey. (See Numbers 22.) The Lord's anger was aroused against Balaam because he disobeyed the Lord's instruction to him. The Angel of the Lord was dispatched to bring judgment to Balaam. Three times God opened the donkey's eyes to see the Angel of the Lord waiting to slay Balaam in his path. Only after the Lord allowed the donkey to *actually speak* to Balaam did the Lord open the eyes of Balaam to see what was happening. Once Balaam's eyes were opened, the Angel of the Lord told him that if he had continued in the path that he was going, the Angel of the Lord would surely have killed him. This is a perfect example of the woes of the Lord. God warns us so that we can turn from our wicked ways and get on the right path. As a spiritual stop sign, a woe can save our lives from unnecessary accidents that could be avoided. People who continue to ignore the warnings of God go through things that they really did not have to go through. We must hear the words of the prophets even when they are prophesying about more than houses and cars and blessings. We must give our ears to prophetic woes.

Like Kermit the frog who often said, "It's not easy being green," *it's not always easy to be a prophet.* Hosea prophesied that prophets would be considered crazy, foolish fanatics!

> The days of visitation and punishment have come; the days of recompense have come; Israel shall know it. The prophet is [considered] a crazed fool and the man who is inspired is [treated as if] mad or a fanatic, because of the abundance of your iniquity and because the enmity, hostility, and persecution are great. Ephraim was [intended to be] a watchman with my God [and a prophet to the surrounding nations]; but he, that prophet, has become a fowler's snare

in all his ways. There is enmity, hostility, and persecution in the house of his God. They have deeply corrupted themselves as in the days of Gibeah. The Lord will [earnestly] remember their iniquity; He will punish their sins. I found Israel like grapes in the wilderness; I saw your fathers as the first ripe fruit on the fig tree in its first season, but they went to Baal-peor and consecrated themselves to that shameful thing [Baal], and they became detestable and loathsome like that which they loved.

—HOSEA 9:7–10, AMP

A prophet is not only called to the gratifying task of foretelling the blessings of God—a prophet is also called to the difficult task of foretelling the judgments of God. When God gives His people warning, it is so that they can have time to repent. One of the prophetic *stop signs* we find in God's Word that is a call to repentance for our nation today is found in 2 Chronicles 7:12–14 (AMP):

And the Lord appeared to Solomon by night and said to him: I have heard your prayer and have chosen this place for Myself as a house of sacrifice. If I shut up heaven so no rain falls, or if I command locusts to devour the land, or if I send pestilence among My people, if My people, who are called by My name, shall humble themselves, pray, seek, crave, and require of necessity My face and turn from their wicked ways, then will I hear from heaven, forgive their sin, and heal their land.

This scripture reveals the fact that God does:

- Shut up heaven so that there is no rain

- Command locusts to devour the land

- Send pestilence among His people

But it also reveals what our response to God's judgment should be. We are advised to:

- Answer the call of God

- Humble ourselves and pray

- Turn from our wicked ways

The good news is that *if we do*, then God will hear our prayers from His throne in heaven, will forgive our sins, and will heal the land!

CHAPTER 10

BE VICTORIOUS
OVER LEGAL ATTACKS

WHEN YOU ARE living for the Lord and the enemy cannot get a foothold in your life, he will attempt to penetrate the peace of your house with legal arrows. The devil is a legalist, and he uses the spirit of litigation to oppress the righteous. He is the accuser of the brethren (Rev. 12:10). This word *accuser* in the Greek is *kategoreo* and means, "to be a plaintiff or the one making the complaint." It also means, "to charge with offense and to always object." The devil is a legalist, and when he is offended, he will always object to those who are the righteous.

The devil will never be aligned with the righteous. If devils are on your side, you may want to check out the side you are on! Satan personally complains about the righteous and makes accusations before the Lord on a consistent basis. If you are doing anything for Jesus, your name will continually be in the mouths of evil men.

This is why the Bible warns us to beware when all men speak well of us.

Though the devil's accusations begin in the spirit, they will eventually manifest in the natural. I have experienced this during my walk with God. I also pray for people around the world who have come under legal attacks that just do not make sense. These attacks will often come one right after the other. I call this kind of warfare, *the demonic dominoes of litigation*. They come to distract and take away the spiritual breath of the target.

Let me explain the term *the target*. It is a spiritual term for *the person under attack*. Up until lately, I have never thought of people becoming literal targets. This can be either spiritual or natural. Recently, I had an encounter with a voodoo priestess who referred to the person she had spiritually manipulated as *the target*. I thought, "Wow, this makes sense. If the devil is shooting arrows, surely he must have targets!" After learning about this, I remembered the Lord telling me that I was *expensive bait* (once when I was under heavy attack). In fishing, bait is used for the targeted catch. With this revelation, what the witch said to me became clearer.

God used the children of Israel to bait the trap for Pharaoh's army in the Red Sea. He used Samson as bait to gather the Philistines in the arena to kill them. The *catch* is the same as the *target*; by using the right kind of bait, the chances are that the catch will be what was *targeted*! Certain kinds of fish tend to go after certain kinds of bait. The devil has a diabolic plan targeted against the elect. These plans can be targeted against individuals, groups, communities, cities, regions, and even nations. This is why the devil always draws lines of separation and division (denominational, racial, political, gender, and cultural lines). He categorizes, divides, and gathers his prey (according to the target), using specific bait that will manifest the catch that he wants.

God showed me that believers who hang out on the walls of warfare and get in the trenches of the front lines have a price on their heads. Though we are *wanted men in the spirit*, we do not live in the demonic paradigms of this world. We are *in the world* but not *of the world*!

As hard as it may be to imagine, the devil really has a hit list of folks he wants to get off his back. These are the believers who give him headaches by praying, fasting, giving, staying in the Word, and, through it all, walking in love. I would rather be on the devil's hit list than God's! Vengeance does belong to the Lord, and men will reap what they have sown!

One of the main arrows the enemy uses is to entrap the righteous through legal snares. Even the traps laid out by hunters have bait in them. Believers have to be able to recognize the bait of the enemy. I believe that this bait comes through spiritual gateways. These gateways can be closed if we love God and hate the world. First John 2:15–16 warns us not to love the world. It clearly states that we cannot love God and love the world.

The opposite of love is hate. We must hate the world! This hate is not the hate described in the hate crimes agenda of today. The kind of hate I am speaking of is one that loves God's commandments to the point whereby we hate anything that comes against them. We should love homosexuals but hate homosexuality. We should love the people doing the acts against God but hate what they do! This script in 1 John also teaches that all that is in the world is:

- The lust of the flesh

- The lust of the eyes

- The pride of life

These are the demonic gateways the enemy uses to bait people, even the elect. He comes through these openings to build cases against the saints. Daniel 7:25 says he will "speak great words against the most High, and shall wear out the saints of the most high, and think to change times and laws" (KJV). The Bible indicates that this will go on for a while, and then darkness will be judged. Glory to God!

Darkness always tries to build a case against the light. The devil's purpose is to wear us out, make us hopeless, and cause us to give up. The good news is that the light is more powerful than darkness. When it comes on the scene, darkness must flee!

This chapter is dedicated to children of the light. I salute you for your commitment to righteousness. The Bible says your afflictions will be many, but God will deliver you from all of them (Ps. 34:19). When you are under attack, always remember that God is up to something bigger and better than the devil's arrows. He uses the arrows of the enemy to sharpen and strengthen us. When the battle is over, no matter what the outcome is in the natural, we come out sharper and stronger in the spiritual. I truly believe that we will not understand how powerful some of our victories were in this life until we go to heaven.

There are some legal attacks that we must go through, and there are others that must be bound at the inception of the attack. The information in this chapter will equip you to deal with both. If the enemy is attacking your household with dominoes of demonic litigation, after reading this chapter you will not be ignorant of his devices.

THE SPIRIT OF INJUSTICE

The Bible warns us that there will be days when right is called wrong and wrong is declared right. Isaiah released a warning to those who did this. Isaiah 5:20 says: "Woe to those who call evil good, and good evil." He goes further by saying that some people exchange "darkness for light, and light for darkness," and "put bitter for sweet, and sweet for bitter."

The scripture says that people who do these things are, "wise in their own eyes" (v. 21). They justify the wicked for reward, and take "away the righteousness of the righteous from him" (v. 23, KJV).

How can a man take away the righteousness of another man? This can easily be done through natural and spiritual legal attacks. For example, a religious person with a legalistic spirit can take away the righteousness of a young lady who is a new believer because of what she wears. He takes away her righteousness in his own mind because of his ideas about what is righteous. In actuality, a righteous person's righteousness cannot be taken away. Our righteousness is in Jesus. It can only be taken away in the accuser's mind.

I praise God that the Book of Isaiah says that a day will come when *Jesus will execute judgment and justice in the earth* (Isa. 16:3). In the meantime, we must stand in truth; if we do, we will be delivered from the attacks of darkness.

The following scriptures will equip you against legal attacks from the enemy. (These verses are taken from the Amplified Bible translation.)

- *Isaiah 43:25*—God has blotted out and canceled our transgressions (for His sake) and does not remember our sins. When the accuser of the brethren attempts to pull evidence up on us from our past, this scripture will shut his mouth.

- *Isaiah 43:26*—God reminds us to: "Put Me in remembrance [remind Me of your merits]; let us plead and argue together," and "Set forth your case, that you may be justified (proved right)."

- *Isaiah 45:25*—"In the Lord shall all the offspring of Israel be justified (enjoy righteousness, salvation, and victory)."

- *Isaiah 50:4*—"The Lord has given Me the tongue of a disciple and of one who is taught." We know how to "speak a word in season to him who is weary."

- *Isaiah 50:5*—"The Lord God has opened My ear, and I have not been rebellious or turned backward."

- *Isaiah 50:6*—"I gave my back to the smiters and My cheeks to those who plucked off the hair; I hid not My face from shame and spitting."

- *Isaiah 50:7*—"For the Lord God helps Me: therefore have I not been ashamed or confounded. Therefore have I set My face like a flint, and I know that I shall not be put to shame."

- *Isaiah 50:8*—"He is near Who declares Me in the right. Who will contend with Me? Let us stand forth together! Who is My adversary? Let him come near to Me."

As we meditate on these passages, Isaiah 59:4 is the icing on the cake. It warns us that:

> No one calls for justice,
> Nor does any plead for truth.
> They trust in empty words and speak lies;
> They conceive evil and bring forth iniquity.

Isaiah relates activities of this sort to the spirit called *cockatrice* (Isa. 59:5). This spirit hatches eggs, and anyone who eats of these eggs dies. It also weaves the spider's web to entangle its prey, and from that which is crushed a viper breaks out.

I have studied the cockatrice spirit for many years. My interest was raised when I found that Isaiah uses it as a spiritual analogy. Apparently this mythological creature was important enough for Isaiah to use to make his point. It is said to have a head, legs, and wings like a cock, but a body and tail like a serpent. The danger of the creature was that it was said to have the power to kill a person who looked into its eyes with one glance. I believe that this is a spirit that needs to be dealt with when we are under legal attack. Let's look at the manifestations of this spirit spoken of in Isaiah 59:6–15:

- Their webs will not become garments (v. 6).

- They will not cover themselves with their works (v. 6).

- Their works are works of iniquity (v. 6).

- The act of violence is in their hands (v. 6).

- Their feet run to evil (v. 7).

- They rush to shed innocent blood (v. 7).

- They think thoughts of iniquity (v. 7).

- Waste and destruction are in their path (v. 7).

- They have never known the way of peace (v. 8).

- There is no justice in their ways (v. 8).

- They make crooked paths for themselves (v. 8).

- Whoever walks in their ways will not know peace (v. 8).

- They cause justice to be far away (v. 9).

- Righteousness will not overtake those in their way (v. 9).

- Those in their way will look for light but find only darkness (v. 9).

- They will wait for brightness but walk in darkness (v. 9).

- They will grope like someone who has no eyes (v. 10).

- They will stumble at noonday as in the night (v. 10).

- They will be like dead men in desolate places (v. 10).

- They will roar like bears and mourn like doves (v. 11).

- They will look for judgment, but there is none (v. 11).

- Salvation will be far away (v. 11).

- Their transgressions are multiplied before the Lord, and their sins will testify against them (v. 12).

- Their transgressions will remain with them, and they will know their iniquities (v. 12).

- They will transgress and lie against the Lord (v. 13).

- They have departed from God (v. 13).

- They speak of oppression and revolt (v. 13).

- They conceive and utter words of falsehood from their hearts (v. 13).

- Justice is turned backward (v. 14).

- Righteousness stands far off (v. 14).

- Although truth has fallen in the streets, equity cannot enter (v. 14).

- Therefore, truth fails (v. 15).

- Those who depart from their evil become their prey (v. 15).

These are the manifestations of an antichrist system that is rooted in secular humanism. The mind-blinding spirit that under-girds this demonic attack is the strongman called *Cockatrice*. As men look into the eyes of this demon, they cannot see truth, right is perverted, and wrong is celebrated.

But there is good news—Isaiah 59:15 says that the Lord saw it and was displeased that there was no judgment! How can the righteous prevail when the system is rooted in a corrupt system with no true judgment? Verse 16 gives the answer—it happens through *intercession*! Read Isaiah 59:16–21 (AMP):

> And He saw that there was no man and wondered that there was no intercessor [no one to intervene on behalf of truth and right]; therefore His own arm brought Him victory, and His own righteousness [having the Spirit without measure] sustained Him. For [the Lord] put on righteousness as a breastplate or coat of mail, and salvation as a helmet upon His head; He put on garments of vengeance for clothing and was clad with zeal [and furious divine jealousy] as a cloak. According as their deeds deserve, so will He repay wrath to His adversaries, recompense to His enemies; on the foreign islands and coastlands He will make compensation. So [as the result of the Messiah's intervention] they shall [reverently] fear the name of the Lord from the west, and His glory from the rising of the sun. When the enemy shall come in like a flood, the Spirit of the Lord will lift up a standard against him and put him to flight [for He will come like a rushing stream which the breath of the Lord drives]. He shall come as a Redeemer to Zion and to those in Jacob (Israel) who turn from transgression, says the Lord. As for Me, this is My covenant or league with them, says the Lord: My Spirit, Who is upon you [and Who writes the law of God inwardly on the heart], and My words which I have put in your mouth shall not depart out of your mouth, or out of the mouths of your

[true, spiritual] children, or out of the mouths of your children's children, says the Lord, from henceforth and forever.

Even in corrupt systems of the world, the righteous prevail. The High Court of Heaven trumps the Supreme Court of the land. The Lord has positioned godly people throughout the system of the world to fight for the things of His kingdom. The abominations of courts, corrections, probation and parole, and law enforcement do not go unnoticed. The Lord sees it all. According to their deeds they will pay. In the meantime, we must be laborers (with God) to stand in the gap against the injustices of the world. Legal and political oppression is under our feet, but we must stand to put spiritual pressure on the powers that be so that we can experience justice in our homes and in the streets of our cities.

PRAYER TARGETS AGAINST LEGAL ATTACKS

Listed below are prayer targets that you can use against legal attacks.

1. Break the assignment of legal weariness.

2. Cancel the petitions of the accuser and command them to be thrown out.

3. Declare the counselors of the wicked incompetent.

4. Bind the Baal Peors of litigation.

5. Come up against evil judgments.

6. Hang the jury of darkness.

7. Petition the high court of appeals (take it to the top).

8. Confess that the spiritual legal fees of your case have been paid off by the blood of Jesus.

9. Shut the traffic controlled by demonic gatekeepers and litigators.

10. Shine the magnificent light of Jesus Christ on every dark verdict.

11. Cancel the deals of conspiracies and confederacies from hell.

12. Bind and cast out every squatting spirit and trespassing demon.

13. Let the track record of your accusers bring shame on them.

14. Ignite the atmosphere of justice and righteousness.

15. Curse everything that calls good, evil and evil, good (right, wrong and wrong, right).

16. Stand and declare your case before the Court of courts and the Judge of judges.

17. Confess that the angels of the Lord will stand against the demonic dominoes of lawsuits.

18. Confess that the enemy has no room in your life and has no case against you.

19. Come up against and remove every file in hell that is maintained against you in the *akashic* records.

20. Release the spear of the Lord to penetrate the truth and overturn every lie against you.

21. Declare that the High Court of Heaven trumps the Supreme Court of the earth.

22. Prophesy to the stairway to heaven and declare that the angels will bring what you need in your case and take away what is not needed.

23. Command the legal arrows of the enemy to become boomerangs and return to their point of origination.

24. Bind legal infractions and distractions with the gavel of God.

25. Declare that the vacuum of the Lord will pull all demonic litigation back into the vortexes of hell.

26. Stand on your legal rights as a believer and confess that what Jesus did on the cross settles the matter and closes your case. Confess that you possess the keys of David. What God locks up cannot be opened, and what He opens cannot be shut.

How to Deal With the Spirit of Litigation

As I was in prayer about this chapter and how believers need to deal with the spirit of litigation, the Lord gave me these things. Deal with:

- Legal booby traps

- The spirit of sabotage

- Demonic entrapments

- The entanglements of litigation

- Defamation of character

- Issues of libel

- The spirit of lies

- Problems of slander

- Demonic liability

- Legal attacks, challenges, and concerns

- Squatter spirits

- Trespassing spirits

- False witnesses

- Spirits that cause false incrimination

- Demonic probation (freedom with strings attached)

- Spiritual halfway houses (no freedom in your own home)

- Dark counsel

- Intellectual counsel

- Counsel of dark conspiracies

- Counsel of dark confederacies

- The counsel of hell

- The counsel of the world

- The counsel of the flesh

- The seat of the ungodly

- The counsel of the wicked

- The parole board of hell

- Demonic indictment

- Demons of anti-appeal assignments against the righteous

- Legal distractions

- Legal torment

- Legal oppression

- Legal depression

- Legal bondage

- Legal soul ties

- Legal old ties

- Ancient spirits of legal infractions

- Ancestral curses of litigation

- The python of legalism and legality

- The *Kosmokrator* (god of this world) over legal darkness

- The cloak of the cosmetic system that covers dark cases

- The cloak that hides the truth

- The principalities that rule over legal jurisdictions and circuits

- Legal attacks from IRS (and other organized systems that promote persecution)

- Financial litigation

- Lawsuit snares and traps

- The judgment of the Sadducees and Pharisees

- The judgment of the Council of 13

- The judgment of the Illuminati

- The judgment of the ungodly

- The judgment of the unrighteous

- The judgment of witches and warlocks

- The judgment of familiar spirits and those who have been trusted but will testify against you

- Territorial spirits of litigation

- Illegal jurisdiction and trespassing spirits

- Unlawful enforcement of laws

- Demonic misinterpretation of laws

- Spirits that disrespect and defy the laws of God

- Spiritual imprisonment

- Demonic solitary confinement

- The hoodwink spirit (mind-blinding, binding spirit)

- Spiritual wickedness in high places

- Dark thrones of authority

- Usurpers of authority

- Gods of revenge

- Gods of backlash

- Gods of retaliation

- Princes of persecution

- Princes of evil prosecution

- Hung juries against the favor of the righteous

- Cases settled against the righteous in the dream life

- Demonic sentences in the dream life

- The spirit of Judas that would sell out his/her clients

- Personal lawsuits

- Business lawsuits

- Lawsuits against the ministry

- Lawsuits on the job

- Employment persecution and discrimination

- Legal attacks against the mind

- (Unlawful) lawsuits between believers

- Spiritual lawsuits

- The little foxes of litigation

- The little leaven of litigation

- Nit-picking legal infractions

- Demonic archive litigation (old cases, old places, old people, old things)

- Religious legalism

- Legal recidivism

- Dark dominoes of litigation

- The demonic threefold cord of no mercy, no grace, no justice (Angels of mercy, grace and justice...*be loosed in Jesus's name!*)

- Clandestine agreements working behind the scenes

- The influence of cults and the occult in the court system

- The interference of witchcraft in our court system, which includes:
  - Voodoo/hoodoo
  - Wicca magic
  - New Age interference
  - White magic, candle magic, black magic
  - Divination
  - Santeria and Yorùbá witchcraft
  - Sorcery and enchantment
  - Familiar spirits
  - Third eyes that rule over jurisdictions
  - Courtroom conjurers

- Caging incantations and lay lines assigned to court sessions

- The empty-shell judge

- Theosophy

- Theomancy

- And every other kind of influence or manipulation of cases that bring negative judgments against the saints

Closing Prayer

Your assignments are broken forever! Every negative verdict settled in cases that concern the elect is overruled and appealed. It is taken to the top of the stairway to heaven (the roche*) and counted as null and void. The High Court of Creation overrules your decision. Your legal rights have been banned and declared illegal. The judicial punishment of the Most High God is against you. If you are an enemy of Jesus Christ, you will reap the highest penalty in the Book of Life. The agreement of light is working against you, and all darkness must flee! Only a righteous decision can be made on the behalf of God's anointed ones. Amen.*

Conclusion

Micah 6:8 says that:

He has shown you, O man, what is good;
And what does the Lord require of you
But to do justly,
To love mercy,
And to walk humbly with your God?

Matthew 12:37 says that we are justified or condemned *by our words*. Idle words will follow us for the rest of our lives. That which is high and esteemed among men is an abomination in the sight of God (Luke 16:15). Romans 2:13 also says that we are not justified by *hearing* the law, but by being *doers* of the law. We are justified by faith (Rom. 5:1) and by the blood of Jesus (Rom. 5:9). God is the One who justifies men (Rom. 8:33). His Word is true, and every man a liar, that we might be justified in our sayings and overcome when we are judged (Rom. 3:4). If God is for us, who can be against us? (See Romans 8:31.) Those God has *predestined*, He also *called*. Those He called, He also *justified*. Those He justified, He also *glorified*—in Jesus's name! (See Romans 8:30.)

CHAPTER 11

GET THE RELIGIOUS SPIRIT
OUT OF YOUR HOUSE

ONE OF THE major spirits that initiates attacks against the church does not come from the darkness of the occult. It does not operate through incantations, voodoo, or rituals. This spirit operates boldly and upfront in the church on a daily basis. It is the *religious spirit*! I mentioned my first obvious encounter with a religious spirit in one of my previous books. As the years passed, I have reached a better understanding of this spirit and how it operates.

A family brought a lady to my husband and me for deliverance at the church on Steele and Blue Street in Jacksonville, Florida. We did not have deliverance teams at the time; the team was Ardell and me. The lady was driven from a mental hospital in South Florida. As God is my witness, when I pulled up to the church, she was sitting in a car—and the car was literally rocking. As she got out of the car, the demons were speaking through her:

"Kim cannot cast me out!"

"Benny Hinn cannot even cast me out!"

"You have never met this demon!"

We went downstairs to the basement of the church where there was no air conditioner in the heat of summer. The lady paced back and forth across the floor, speaking in demonic voices and declaring that we had no power to cast the demon out. She said:

"You cannot cast me out!"

"I pray in tongues just like you!"

"I quote scriptures like the Son of God!"

And then she uttered words that I will never forget...

"I AM THE RELIGIOUS SPIRIT!"

I thought, "My God, religious—*spirit*?" Though the words of this woman baffled my intellect, the devil had been set up. This was the worst thing this stupid devil could have ever done. He revealed his identity and blew his cover in the church! At the time, my natural mind could not relate religion to a demon. But because of the intensity of what we were experiencing with this lady, by faith we began to call some of the manifestations of religion out. We called out:

- The spirit that gives offerings to be seen or looks for something in return

- The spirit that likes to be in charge in the church

- The spirit of perversion that comes with religion through false holiness

- The spirit that dresses up the demonic with church clothes (long dresses, veils, no pants, head coverings)

- The spirit that gets in the choir and praise teams

- The Scripture-quoting demon

- The spirit of condemnation

- The form of godliness

- The church-splitting demon

- The spirit of the false calling

- Spiritual adultery

- The spirit of the clique

- The spirit that oppress the youth and turns them from God

- The spirit that prays in false tongues

- The false, shouting spirit that releases witchcraft in the church through the work of the flesh

- Charismatic witchcraft that cloaks the anointing through men's gifts

- The spirit of false prophecy

- The anti-evangelistic spirit

- The spirit of arrested development over a ministry

- The family (familiar spirit) demon

These are examples of a few of many things that can be called out of a person who needs deliverance from a religious spirit. The most important thing in this delivery is that the minister be *Spirit led*. Calling the wrong thing at the wrong time (out of a person) can sometimes shut that person down, and he or she will not be open for deliverance. Other spirits include:

- The spirit that worships titles

- The spirit of false revival

- The demon called Overspirituality

- The spirit of the law (that can never be kept)

The good news is that the religious spirit was cast out of that woman (at Steel and Blue) years ago, and since that time we have cast out more than we can count. The bad news is that many believers are still in the same place of ignorance that I once was. They cannot relate *religion* to a *demon*, or *Charismatic* to *witchcraft*.

The key thing to remember is that the root of all power comes from God. There is no power in creation that did not originate through the Creator. Powers of darkness are only twisted and perverted forms of the original power of our God. This is why all witches and others from the dark side use Scripture, religious books, and religious symbolism to do their dirty deeds.

A scary thing to me is that the religious spirit cloaks itself under the guise of true spirituality in Christ. Most believers cannot discern it. It is my prayer that this chapter will remove scales and veils from the eyes of God's people. The enemy is launching an inside attack against the church. He will use praise, prophecy, the gifts, or even the Word of God against us. Remember, *for everything that God created*, the devil *duplicated a counterfeit*.

Religion in the Word of God

Let's take a look at the Word of God and what it says about religion.

> Then Agrippa said to Paul, You are permitted to speak on your own behalf. At that Paul stretched forth his hand and made his defense [as follows]: I consider myself fortunate, King Agrippa, that it is before you that I am to make my defense today in regard to all the charges brought against

me by [the] Jews, [especially] because you are so fully and unusually conversant with all the Jewish customs and controversies; therefore, I beg you to hear me patiently. My behavior and manner of living from my youth up is known by all the Jews; [they are aware] that from [its] commencement my youth was spent among my own race in Jerusalem. They have had knowledge of me for a long time, if they are willing to testify to it, that in accordance with the strictest sect of our religion I have lived as a Pharisee. And now I stand here on trial [to be judged on the ground] of the hope of that promise made to our forefathers by God, which hope [of the Messiah and the resurrection] our twelve tribes confidently expect to realize as they fervently worship [without ceasing] night and day. And for that hope, O king, I am accused by Jews and considered a criminal!

Why is it thought incredible by any of you that God raises the dead? I myself indeed was [once] persuaded that it was my duty to do many things contrary to and in defiance of the name of Jesus of Nazareth. And that is what I did in Jerusalem; I [not only] locked up many of the [faithful] saints (holy ones) in prison by virtue of authority received from the chief priests, but when they were being condemned to death, I cast my vote against them. And frequently I punished them in all the synagogues to make them blaspheme; and in my bitter fury against them, I harassed (troubled, molested, persecuted) and pursued them even to foreign cities. Thus engaged I proceeded to Damascus with the authority and orders of the chief priests.

— ACTS 26:1–12, AMP

This passage of Scripture confirms that since the beginning of the church, the enemy has been using believers to persecute one another in the church. One of the main ways to recognize the work of religious spirits is this: *Under the disguise of religion, it persecutes the righteous and faithful.*

Paul makes a clear distinction between his time growing up as a leader under the law of the church and his born-again experience after he met Christ on the road to Damascus. The road to Damascus represents more than the dramatic conversion of Paul's life. It also reveals the plot of the enemy to persecute and trouble God's elect from within the church.

Galatians 1:13–14 (AMP) reads:

> You have heard of my earlier career and former manner of life in the Jewish religion (Judaism), how I persecuted and abused the church of God furiously and extensively, and [with fanatical zeal did my best] to make havoc of it and destroy it. And [you have heard how] I outstripped many of the men of my own generation among the people of my race in [my advancement in study and observance of the laws of] Judaism, so extremely enthusiastic and zealous I was for the traditions of my ancestors.

Through his own testimony, Paul reveals that *the traditions of men are the strongholds of religion.*

> In vain (fruitlessly and without profit) do they worship Me, ordering and teaching [to be obeyed] as doctrines the commandments and precepts of men. You disregard and give up and ask to depart from you the commandment of God and cling to the tradition of men [keeping it carefully and faithfully].
>
> —MARK 7:7–8, AMP

This passage highlights vain worship. Vain worship is like a person going to the gym seven days a week and working out with no results. God says that vain worship produces no results. This is why many people accept defeat in God and backslide. If this is you, the word of the Lord unto you is that *there is no failure in Christ!* This can be manifested in our lives if we give high regard to the commandments of the Lord and take our attention off of the traditions of men.

The traditions of men flow through *generational religious spirits.*

People literally pick up religious habits that have nothing to do with the commandments of the Lord and are more faithful to them than to the Word of God.

Colossians 2:6–23 teaches on freedom from human regulations through a new birth in Christ. It warns us of man-made traditions and the principles of this world. Verse 14 speaks of the cancellation of "the written code" and its regulations. This code worked against the believer in Christ and not for him. It made people set unattainable goals that gave birth to the fruit of failure, defeat, and misery. It literally opposed the abundant freedom in Christ that was meant to be. Galatians 5:1 commands that we stand fast in the liberty by which Christ has made us free. It goes on to say that we should not be entangled again with the yoke of bondage.

It is important that we research the Greek meaning of the following words:

- "Stand fast" (*steko*)—To stand firm in faith and duty; to have a constant flow that causes one to persevere.

- "Liberty" (*eleutheria*)—To be blessed with generosity and independence that is bestowed upon a person as a result of the economy of God's grace, which was not made available under the Law of the Old Testament. To also have independence from religious regulation that is rooted in the legal restrictions of man.

James 2:10–14 (AMP) teaches on the *Perfect Law of Liberty*. Let's read:

> For whosoever keeps the Law [as a] whole but stumbles and offends in one [single instance] has become guilty of [breaking] all of it. For He Who said, You shall not commit adultery, also said, You shall not kill. If you do not commit adultery but do kill, you have become guilty of transgressing the [whole] Law. So speak and so act as [people should]

who are to be judged under the law of liberty [the moral instruction given by Christ, especially about love]. For to him who has shown no mercy the judgment [will be] merciless, but mercy [full of glad confidence] exults victoriously over judgment. What is the use (profit), my brethren, for anyone to profess to have faith if he has no [good] works [to show for it]? Can [such] faith save [his soul]?

There is no liberty in Jesus Christ without mercy. During the past eight months, the Lord has been speaking to me with instructions to *sow seeds of mercy and grace, because we reap only what has been sown!* It would be a terrible thing to need mercy or grace, and to not have sown either. Religious people and their settings have zero balances in their spiritual accounts when it comes to mercy. The passage above says that those who show no mercy will be merciless. The Perfect Law of Liberty declares that mercy is victorious over judgment. The key word is balance. Judgment is a serious thing, but even the judgment of God is undergirded with mercy. If we look hard enough, somewhere in God's judgments we will find His incredible mercy.

- "Entangled" (*enecho*)—To be held subject to or be under the control of. To struggle over, quarrel with or go back and forth with.

- "Yoke" (*zygos*)—That which attaches two things together like oxen pulling a load. It couples things and causes them to be connected by a hard burden to bear.

- "Bondage" (*douleia*)—Servitude that promotes dependence upon a person, place, or thing; the state of a man that prevents from freely possessing abundant life and enjoying it

Based on the Greek definitions for the words "entangled in a yoke of bondage," it can be determined that anything that causes a believer to struggle or be double-minded about a thing to the point that person becomes attached to a burdensome load and prevented from enjoying the abundant life that Christ died for is not of God, but is devilish. To sum it up in a nutshell—the spirit of religious bondage is demonic.

Many believers are stuck in ruts whereby they are not experiencing new growth in Christ Jesus. When there is true *new birth*, it must be confirmed with *new growth*. The genuine new birth experience causes old things to be cut off and passed away. Once the old is pruned, the new can grow. If a believer continues to return to the old yoke of bondage, he or she will be bound by spiritually arrested development. They will not experience the level-to-level, glory-to-glory promised to them in the Word of God. They will be condemned to a form of godliness, which makes a person appear to be victorious in Jesus on the outside. But in actuality, they will shut down the power on the inside of them that is greater than what is coming against them in life. There is no victory in the life of the believer who succumbs to the regiments, rudiments, and habits of religious forms.

CHARACTERISTICS OF RELIGIOUS SPIRITS

I would like to close this chapter out by listing a few practical characteristics of religious spirits and how they can be recognized.

1. Religious spirits have no authority in Jesus Christ. Jesus hated religious spirits. Jesus was not a religious person, and He did things that shook the religious kingdoms of the earth. Acts 19:13–16 tells the story of seven sons of a man named Sceva. They were referred to as "vagabond Jews and exorcists." In

other words, they were religious. The story reveals that they had no power over unclean spirits.

2. Religion steals the youthful joy of young people in serving Jesus; it makes the elders become demonically *old*. In Matthew 19:14, Jesus forbid His disciples from stopping the little children from coming to Him. I do not believe in an *age of spiritual accountability*. Everything that has breath must praise and serve the Lord (Ps. 150:6). Children must be raised up in the things of God so that they will not depart.

   The Bible only has one account whereby a prophet is called "old." In the Book of 1 Kings, a man from Judah prophesied against the altar at Bethel. The king ordered that the man from Judah be seized. The king's arm froze as he pointed to the prophet from Judah, and the king could not pull his arm back to himself. The king asked the man from Judah to pray that his arm would be healed. He prayed, and the king was healed. Rumors of the authority of the prophet from Judah spread, and he was summoned by an "old prophet." This prophet was not necessarily old in age but actually washed up. He was spiritually or demonically old! (See 1 Kings 13.)

3. Religion is an anti-evangelism spirit. Matthew 23:15 warns the religious sects of the church that they lose more souls than they win. Their converts become doubly as hellish as them.

4. Religion is antichrist. Religious people (the Pharisees and the Sadducees) killed Jesus.

5. Religious people have no joy and, ultimately, *no power*! Nehemiah 8:10 declared that the joy of the Lord is our strength. It denotes that the person who lives in the dwelling place of the Lord (the place of joy—in the presence of the Lord there is fullness of joy) is reinforced with power.

6. Religious spirits breed bondage and condemnation and block true liberty. (See Galatians 5:1; Romans 8:1.)

7. Religion creates a form of godliness through regimen and repetition. Second Timothy 3:5 warns us to avoid people with forms of godliness.

8. Religion corrupts and perverts. It promotes an unrealistic standard that cannot be obtained because of the dictates of the flesh. This is why true worshipers worship in spirit and in truth. The law was a schoolmaster that taught us that in and of our fleshly natures, we cannot obey the commandments of God. This is why we were given a new (and better) covenant. The laws of God are now written in our hearts and not on tablets of stone. Trying to live by the dictates of the tablets of stone alone only opens the doors to corruption and perversion through *religious spirits of failure*. This is why perversion and corruption are multiplied when men attempt to serve God by their own power and by their guidelines. (See Hebrews 8:7–13.)

9. Religion stems from the root of spiritual schizophrenia. One minute the people blessed the name

of the Lord and cried, "Hosanna to the Highest!" In another breath they yelled, "Crucify Him!"

10. Religion hinders positive relationships by putting a bad taste in the mouths of unbelievers, taking the fire out of marriages, stopping the flow of God in worship fellowships, and making children hate serving God.

To sum it all up, judgment will start at the house of God. Remember, it was religious spirits that nailed Jesus to the cross. Let us not religiously or repetitively serve God. We must worship Him in spirit and in truth. Selah!

CHAPTER 12

THE SCIENCE OF GOD

A FEW WEEKS AGO I was helping my twelve-year-old twins with their science homework. Because my children are home-schooled and use only a Bible-based curriculum, I could easily see the difference in the concept of the world in reference to science versus the truth (which is only in God).

The lesson that we studied that day shook my soul. I began to see the strategy the enemy used to take God out of science. You may ask the question, "Why is the topic of science important in a spiritual warfare book on spiritual housekeeping?" The answer to that question is easy. Let's look first at the meaning of the word *science*. It comes from the Latin word *scientia*, and it means, "to have knowledge." All of the occult organizations of the world root their strength in knowledge. As believers, we are confident that our strength is in God. But in this strength, He gives us the knowledge we need to excel in every area of our lives.

Some time ago, I listened to a message by a powerful man of God who taught that the way we think creates an environment; and an environment that is maintained over a period of time becomes a climate. The definition of a *climate* is "the prevailing conditions of a place that determines everything about it."

A spiritual climate produces attitudes, standards, moods, tones, temperaments, and even the spirit of a place. Once a climate is established, it becomes a stronghold. For example, many islands are known for tropical climates. Alaska is known to be one of the coldest places in the world (a winter climate). This is established through the conditions that have prevailed over the years. There are winter and tropical strongholds.

Another example is a stronghold that I have noticed to rule over Atlanta, Georgia. From personal observation, I believe that Atlanta has become a stronghold for African American homosexual men, much like San Francisco is a stronghold for homosexuals in general. Before all of these men came out of the closet or persisted to be undercover homosexuals (on the *down-low*), an ideology or mind-set had to become prevalent. A few gay people cannot produce a climate of perversion. It takes many minds thinking the same thing to produce an atmosphere. Even the Word of the Lord says that one person can put a thousand to flight and two people can put ten thousand to flight (Deut. 32:30). There is power in agreement, even in thought—it sets the atmosphere!

Godly standards can be torn down and ungodly ones built up in a home, community, city, nation, or church. This displacement of righteousness with unholy things or ungodly acts can cause people to be under strongholds that produce temperaments and mind-sets that have never existed. The most dangerous thing about a stronghold is the deception of it. A person can live in a stronghold all of his or her life and not be aware of it. The deception of the stronghold is familiarity. People can become so familiar with a thing that *the thing* can become unrecognizably or unnoticeably wrong.

Strongholds literally guard over climates that make right seem wrong and wrong seem right. Once a stronghold is established, anyone under the power of the stronghold is directly connected to second-heaven activity. The prince of the power of the air (Eph. 2:2) operates behind the scenes as the puppet master of these climates. Eventually the people in these strongholds begin to do things without thinking about them, because an attitude is set in place. Their minds have been blinded, and their actions become the norm.

As human beings, we witness the manifestation of things but tend to not pay attention to their origination. Where does the idea of a man being a woman or a woman being a man originate? What would make a little girl who grew up as a virgin in a godly home go away to college and take on the temperament of a loose woman? I believe that these things come from thoughts that attach themselves to the minds of individuals. Strongholds reinforce themselves through repetition. The *thoughts* keep coming, and the *acts* continue to be seen until they *are accepted*. Thus the demonic cycle is completed.

Strongholds hide under the demonic covering of lies. These lies keep people from knowing the truth, because ultimately only the truth can free them from the stronghold. Let me give you an example of how a demonic atmosphere was set in a major church in America.

The pastor was an international speaker. She asked for my advice about meeting with a large group of people from the homosexual agenda in her church. The group was harassing her church because she was not an advocate of same-sex marriage. The pastor wanted to invite them for dinner and *have dialogue* with them.

I told her that I would be praying for her, but I would not advise the meeting in her church. She did meet with them and called me a few weeks later to discuss her regret for doing it. In the natural there were no concerns. But demonic things took place in the spirit. She explained that the atmosphere in her church had not been the same since the meeting. She even admitted having thoughts come to her mind that she had never had before. By God's grace and mercy, it was an atmosphere she *did not allow to be sustained* long enough to complete the demonic cycle. The church was cleaned out, and the pastor learned a great lesson.

Another pastor friend allowed a traveling preacher to minister to his congregation. The traveling preacher took an offering for tens of thousands of dollars. The congregation was not that large. There is nothing wrong with taking up large offerings, but something was not right about this traveling preacher. The pastor admitted that the atmosphere in his church changed, and the church began to have financial challenges. It was months before his church could break the power of the dark atmosphere that had been set and be restored.

These are testimonies that came out with positive endings. But it is scary to think of how many churches, homes, and marriages have come under demonic attack and never recovered! This is why we have to keep ideologies, mind-sets, and ways of doing things that do not line up with God out of the places over which we have been given stewardship.

THE STRONGHOLD OF EDUCATION

The enemy has been infiltrating the minds of our people through the education system. This is why home schools and private schools with moral standards are so important. To keep the atmospheres of our homes spiritually healthy, we must pay attention to where and how our children are being educated. Many people take pride in attending schools like Harvard and Yale. Yet these schools are breeding grounds for ideologies that are antichrist and pro-devil. Many of the instructors are giving more than information and knowledge; they are training minds! A mind is a terrible thing to waste. It is a waste of a mind to educate a person without including instruction about the One who created them. Training up a mind (in a child) in the way that he or she should go can be biblical or demonic. Getting knowledge is not enough; in all our getting, the Bible says we need to get understanding. We need to know the strongholds that rule over the places where our children go to school every day and every year.

Strongholds can be holy or demonic. There is a ruling or prevailing spirit over every person or place. The type of ruling spirit over a person or place can be easily discerned by paying attention to *actions*, *atmospheres*, and *climates*. As believers, we just need to *pay attention*, and God will reveal what we need to know. It is the will of God for us to have knowledge, but we must get it in the right way and not at any cost.

Proverbs 18:15 says: "The heart of the prudent acquires knowledge, and the ear of the wise seeks knowledge." In Ecclesiastes 1:16, Solomon communicated the fact that his heart had "understood great wisdom and knowledge." Wisdom and knowledge are twins that must be birthed into the life of every born-again believer. While walking in this wisdom and knowledge, the Lord commands us to be "wise as serpents" (Matt. 10:16).

Finally, it is important to note that the Bible teaches that the children of the world are "more shrewd in their generation" than the children of light (Luke 16:8). What is God saying? Is He saying that the people of the world are more intelligent and wiser than God's people? Absolutely not! This chapter in Luke teaches on the plight of the unjust steward. God is not highlighting unbelievers over believers; however, He is warning His people to be good stewards over what He has given them.

Dangerously misinterpreted spiritual cliché's like "Jesus has done it all" and "Just believe it and receive it" have released a spirit in the church where Christians are not stepping out and *doing* what the Word tells us to do. A deception has been planted into their minds that *just because they are saved*, things will automatically happen for them.

God puts certain gifts in the lives of all people. Every human being has the responsibility to identify their gifting from God and apply it accordingly. If this does not happen, people will never be fulfilled or effective in life. The biblical story of Daniel and the three Hebrew boys is a perfect example of this principle.

> As for these four young men, God gave them knowledge and skill in all literature and wisdom; and Daniel had understanding in all visions and dreams. Now at the end of the days, when the king had said that they should be brought in, the chief of the eunuchs brought them in before Nebuchadnezzar. Then the king interviewed them, and among them all none was found like Daniel, Hananiah, Mishael, and Azariah; therefore they served before the king. And in all matters of wisdom and understanding about which the king examined them, he found them ten times better than all the magicians and astrologers who were in all his realm.
>
> —DANIEL 1:17–20

This passage says that God gave these young men *knowledge and skills in all learning and wisdom*. In other words God:

- Gave them skills

- Gave them knowledge on how to apply those skills

- Gave them wisdom in maintaining the skills

- Did not limit their gifts to the things of His kingdom but extended them to *all learning* concerning the natural kingdom in which they lived.

As a result of God's intervention into their lives, Shadrach, Meshach, Abednego, and Daniel were ten times wiser than all the *learned* magicians and enchanters of the land.

ALL GIFTS
COME FROM GOD

To put everything in a nutshell, *all gifts come from God*. He is the Creator. He created man, the universe, and everything that can possibly occur between the two. What does this have to do with science? Well, it is important to understand the purpose of science. Its purpose is to develop general laws that explain how the world around us works and why things happen the way they do. Because God is the Creator of all things, it is difficult to properly assess how a thing works unless you can interpret the vision that the One who made the thing had for it. In other words, knowledge without God will always lead to erroneous teachings and beliefs. It will form strongholds of thought.

Everything started with God and can only be understood through God. The vision that I have for this chapter is to address the issue of how God is being taken out of things that only He can be the foundation of. We live in a country that is under a stronghold of demonic attack. The strategy is to remove God from the institution of marriage, the foundation of the family, and the core of our government. The enemy ignited a diabolic plan by perverting school subjects like science to create a *man-conscious* society that displaces a *God-conscious* one. A black cloak has been placed over the God-consciousness of America. The devil has hoodwinked instructors who are seeding their ideologies into the minds of the innocent. They teach about a world without a Creator, whereby secular humanism becomes a god. The sad thing is that the generational curse that had been set in place in our education system will one day cause the innocent minds that have been seeded to seed the minds of the next generation of prey.

Joy filled my heart the day that I helped the twins with their science homework. We were studying from schoolbooks that put emphasis on God in a society that has attempted to intentionally leave Him out. It is not too late. The saints must be made aware of the dilemma we face. I have shared the problem, and I am sure that you know that no problem is too big for God. There are more for us than there can ever be against us. In my own research, I discovered that most of the pioneers of scientific breakthroughs were devout believers. There were many scientists who were anti-God, but the amazing fact is that there were many devout believers involved in the foundation of the knowledge we have in our educational system today. Let's look at both sides of the coin.

In the remainder of this chapter we will look at some false, world-centered scientists and the climate they have created. In the next chapter we will meet some *apostles of the science of God*.

FALSE SCIENTISTS

Science has never been one of my favorite subjects, but after studying it from a Bible-based perspective, I was fascinated. The practice of science involves experiments and observations—men observing the things that went on around them and collecting the facts. This can pose somewhat of a problem. The facts that are collected depend on *how men see things* and can be biased. Even though science claims to be *based on proven facts*, the opinions of men as to what is an actual fact has great influence. Let's take a look at the history of science as it relates to key pioneers of scientific study.

Three thousand years before Christ, the Egyptians started practices such as:

- Putting molded bread on open sores (They unknowingly used the penicillin that was produced from the molded bread.)

- Putting poppy seeds on people who were in pain (They unknowingly used the morphine and codeine from the plant.)

- Taking thin slices of the stem from the papyrus plant, moistening it, drying it out, and using it to write on (They are responsible for the invention of what we call *paper* today.)

Though the Egyptians, Mesopotamians, and Chinese were experimenting and observing facts long before anyone else, historians did not recognize their findings as science. Scientists were first acknowledged in 600 B.C. in Greece. The men historically given credit for being humanity's first true scientists are Thales, Anaximander, and Anaximenes. The scientific breakthroughs made by the Egyptians were not recognized as science for twenty-four hundred years when these men were finally given credit. This proves that we need to take a closer look at science as it has been presented to us. Science, as we know it, has generally been controlled by the intellectual minds of men. Anytime intellect is in control, it tends to fight against God and His laws. Romans 8:7 says that the carnal mind is enmity against God. It goes on to say that the carnal mind is not subject to the law of God because it simply cannot be.

It is hard to believe that the three men who are given credit for being the first scientists *all failed in their attempts to prove any hypotheses they posed*. What is wrong with this picture? Thales studied the heavens to interpret the movement of heavenly bodies. Can you imagine someone trying to study the heavens without God? His scientific studies ended up being nothing to write a science chapter about, especially not a book. The most that came out of his studies was the observation of a solar eclipse.

It is thought that Thales mentored Anaximander. This is probably correct, because the generational curse of failure manifested through his studies also. Anaximander is said to be the first man to attempt to prove the origin of man without God. He came up with the theory that life started in the sea and that human life began in the form of a fish. As far as making any sense out of it, or even get-ting a following, his theory bit the dust.

Anaximenes was an associate of Anaximander. He tried to prove that everything was made out of air. Of course that theory fell to the ground, and he was also proven wrong.

Let's take a look at the failing science of Ptolemy. He was the scientist who came up with a so-called discovery that everything in the solar system revolved around the earth (not the sun). His theory did nothing more than cause years of confusion. It was referred to as the *geocentric system* because the earth was the center of everything. When many other scientists proved him wrong, the Catholic Church tried to maintain the geocentric system theory. Their stance was that God was the Creator, and since He created the earth, everything should revolve around it. The problem was that they were nowhere close to the truth about the solar system.

It is important to point out that *the powers that be* made the prac-tice of alchemy an officially noted science. Word IQ.com provides this information about alchemy:

> An early protoscientific practice combining elements of chemistry, physics, astrology, art, semiotics, metallurgy, medicine, mysticism, and religion. There were three main goals many alchemists sought for. The most renowned goal of alchemy is the transmutation of any metal into either gold or silver. Also they tried to create universal panacea, a remedy that would cure all diseases and prolong life indefi-nitely. The philosopher's stone was the key in these goals. This mythical substance, which could just as well be powder or liquid as a stone, had the ability to do both. The third goal was creating human life. Alchemy can be regarded as the precursor of the modern science of chemistry prior to the formulation of the scientific method.
>
> The word *alchemy* comes from the Arabic *al-kimiya* or *al-khimiya*, which is probably formed from the article *al-* and the Greek word *khumeia* meaning "cast together",

"pour together", "weld", "alloy", etc. (from *khumatos*, "that which is poured out, an ingot"). Another widely reported etymology links the word with "Al Kemi", meaning "the Egyptian Art", since Ancient Egyptians called their land "Kemi" and were widely regarded as powerful magicians throughout the ancient world.[1]

Alchemy was more than a science; it was an art—a black art at that. It included magic, mysticism, astrology, and religion (without Jesus). Need I say more about this documented legal form of science? This so-called science opposes the Word of God and is rooted in witchcraft. It is related to the work of the flesh spoken of in Galatians 5:19-21, which identifies all witchcraft as a work of the flesh. The word *witchcraft* is *pharmekia* in the Greek, and it means, "to be magically medicated." The symbol of the alchemists (a pot with a stirring element in it) is on most pharmacies around the world today.

In 2 Kings 18:4, the idol that the Israelites worshiped and burned incense for healing from the time of Moses to the time of Hezekiah was Nehushtan. During this time, it was a pole with a serpent wrapped around it. Today this same symbol is the symbol of the medical field in our country—a pole with a snake wrapped around it.

Just as there can be false apostles and prophets, there can also be false scientists and false systems. Anything that goes against the truth of the Bible is false. There are only two sides in the spirit— light and dark. The Bible is the light, and anything that opposes it is dark. The foundation of all truth must originate from the Word of God and be covered by the blood of Jesus. The foundation of what we call *science* has some bad blood in it. It has been proven that men noted for being the first scientists had no scientific breakthroughs to back up the titles given to them. They are like healing evangelists with no miracles...intercessors without a prayer language...preachers without a word...or prophets without utterance.

They are just false! They are not who they are supposed to be, doing what they are supposed to be doing.

I thank God that the real thing did exist. Not only were there real scientists, but also they were known as *real men of God*. The schoolbooks in America will not mention the faith of these apostles of science, so I would like to introduce you to them in the next chapter.

CHAPTER 13

THE APOSTLES OF THE SCIENCE OF GOD

DURING THE PERIOD of time known as the Dark Ages, scientific progress simply did not exist. The influence of the Roman government discouraged scientific study. The Romans worshiped many gods. They believed that these gods roamed the earth in ultimate authority. Their thought was that the gods controlled everything and that science was of no profitable use. During this age of darkness, Roman Catholic monks gathered and maintained large volumes of scientific observations and speculations. This information eventually became what is known today as *encyclopedias*. These monks and Christians in general (during the Dark Ages) believed that God had revealed Himself to His creation in two ways: through Scripture and through nature.

Because of this, God used them to copy scriptures, scientific data, and ideas to preserve them for future generations. It is because of these men of God that scientists had a foundation to work from after the Dark Ages. It is also important to note that the Christian church was instrumental in continuing the progress of medical treatment during this time. During the Dark Ages, medicine was studied in monasteries because Christians believed it was their duty to minister to the sick.

After A.D. 1000, Christian scholars realized that their beliefs promoted a completely different way of looking at things in the world. They believed in one God who created the universe according to His laws. The essence of their view toward science was:

> The way the world worked could be explained, as long as scientists based it on the natural laws that God had already established.

There are some earlier Christians who were also recognized as men of science. They loved God and believed in a harmony between biblical fact and scientific knowledge—not discord. Although they will be found missing from the schoolbooks of America, I chose to highlight some of these apostles of science in this chapter.

1. **Robert Grosseteste (1175–1253)** was a bishop in the Roman Catholic Church and one of the most learned men of the Middle Ages. Although several scientists have been credited with the creation of the scientific method, including Aristotle, Roger Bacon, and Galileo, Robert Grosseteste's commentary written in the twelfth century on *Posterior Analytics* sets him apart as one of the first scholastic thinkers to understand the dual nature of scientific reasoning. He was deeply interested in scientific method, which he described as both inductive and deductive. He was deeply committed to the idea that the secrets of the natural world could be revealed by God's natural laws.[1]

2. **Roger Bacon (1221–1291)** was a great English friar and philosopher who is hailed by many as the father of modern science. His focus on empirical approaches to science was influential. He was a devout Christian who predicted that science would bring marvels like submarines, flying machines, and explosive and worldwide travel (he was a prophetic scientist). People laughed at him during his time, but time has proven to be his friend. His predictions came to pass. He was also known for attempting to use science to destroy superstition. He wrote *Opus Majus*, one of the earliest encyclopedias.[2]

3. **Thomas Bradwardine (1290–1349)** was a Roman Catholic bishop known for questioning the teachings of Catholicism and known as the first reformer. He emphasized salvation by faith alone, through the grace of God. His theological lectures delivered at Oxford were expanded into a famous treatise on grace known as *Summa Doctoris Profundi*. Luther and Calvin were heavily influenced by his teachings. His reputation as a scholar was also based on his mathematical words. He is often called *Doctor Profundus*, meaning "the Profound Doctor." He used mathematics and scientific experiments to prove that Aristotle's ideas on motion were wrong. Three hundred years after his death, Aristotle's theory was officially discounted.[3]

4. **Nicholas of Cusa (1400–1464)** was a German cardinal and philosopher. He is considered by many to be a genius ahead of his time in the field of science. As a scientist he studied the planets and stars. His findings revolutionized the study of planets.

He proved that the geocentric view of planets was wrong. He was particular interested in the idea that God is infinite. It was said that his curiosity about God's infinite nature motivated him to study the planets of the universe. For Nicholas, the exact center and circumference of the created universe are to be found only in God.[4]

5. **Nicholas Copernicus (1473–1543)**, founder of the *Copernican System*, proved that the sun was the center of the solar system (the Heliocentric system), and that the sun, the earth, and the moon were all shaped like round balls. He was a canon and bishop in the Roman Catholic Church and did a scientific study on planets at the request of the pope. His studies caused the church to publicly denounce his work because it did not support the church's geocentric view. However, Galileo revealed Copernicus's ideas for what they were—a revolution in how humankind conceived of itself. Many marveled that the Creator of a now infinite universe would lavish such attention on a planet that seemed to stand at the periphery of all creation. [5]

6. **Johannes Kepler (1571–1630)** was known as one of the most important compilers of information on the heliocentric view (Helios—the Greek god of the sun). He created the mathematical equations that supported the heliocentric system. He laid the foundation for the fact that all of the planets of the solar system revolve around the sun. Kepler wanted to be a minister, but because of financial difficulties he accepted a job as a teacher. While he taught, he studied the heavens. His hope was

that his observations would bring glory to God. In a letter he wrote, "I wanted to become a theologian. For a long time, I was restless. Now, however, behold how *through my effort God is being celebrated through astronomy.*"[6]

7. **Galileo (1564–1642)** was a part of the Roman Catholic Church. His most famous invention was the telescope, and his scientific discoveries supported the heliocentric view. Because of this, the church tried him in court for heresy. He was a devout member of the church, and he openly renounced his findings. He did keep notes that (after his death) eventually proved too powerful for the Catholic Church. The church eventually had to renounce its view in support of the geocentric system. On October 31, 1992, 350 years after Galileo's death, Pope John Paul II gave an address on behalf of the Catholic Church in which he admitted that errors had been made by the theological advisors in the case of Galileo. He declared the Galileo case closed, but he did not admit that the church was wrong to convict Galileo on a charge of heresy because of his belief that the earth rotates around the sun.[7]

8. **Blaise Pascal (1623–1662)** was known as a brilliant philosopher, mathematician, and scientist; he is also popular for the books he has written on Christian apologetics. He is the author of the famous book *Paschal's Wager.* This book presents a person's worldview in terms of a bet. He argues that Christianity is by far the best bet. Pascal believed that "there is a God-shaped vacuum in the heart

of every man which cannot be filled by any created thing, but only by God the Creator, made known through Jesus Christ."[8] His studies led to what is now known as Pascal's Law. The science behind this law caused the invention of hydraulic lifts.[9]

9. **Sir Isaac Newton (1642–1727)**, known as the greatest scientist in history, discovered the three laws of motion—the binomial theorem, method of fluxions, and his greatest discovery of all, the law of gravitation. He was a great mathematician and created the system of mathematics known as calculus. He formulated a universal law of gravity and also did studies with prisms to prove that white light is really composed of many different colors. He was known as a devout, unorthodox Christian. He studied science specifically as a means of learning more about God. He was said to always highlight the fact that *the best way to study God is through Bible study*. He believed that the Bible is literally true in every respect. Throughout his life, he continually tested biblical truth against the physical truths of experimental and theoretical science. He never observed a contradiction. In fact, he viewed his own scientific work as a method by which to reinforce belief in biblical truth. He wrote many commentaries on the Bible that concentrated on prophecy. In his later years he spent more time writing commentaries on the Book of Daniel than writing about science.[10]

10. **Robert Boyle (1627–1691)** is known as the founder of modern-day chemistry, which was created out of the theory called Boyle's Law. Modern chemistry

owes enormous gratitude to the work and writings of Robert Boyle—a creation scientist whose love of God's truth led him to overcome the chief errors of alchemical theory, which were hindering the development of truly scientific chemistry. Boyle was dedicated to his faith in Christianity and often wrote sermons on nature that gave glory to God. His last words to a group of scientists were, "Remember to give glory to the One Who authored nature."[11]

11. **Antonie Leeuwenhoek (1632–1723)** is commonly known as "the Father of Microbiology" and considered to be the first microbiologist. He is best known for his work on the improvement of the microscope and for his contributions toward the establishment of microbiology. He often referred with reverence to the wonders God designed in making creatures great and small. He believed that his amazing discoveries were merely further proof of the great wonder of God's creation.[12]

12. **Carolus Linnaeus (1707–1778)** was a Swedish botanist, physician, and zoologist who published several volumes with his classifications of all living plants and animals. His well-known book, *Species Plantarum*, published in 1753, contained 1,200 pages and described over 7,300 species.[13] He revolutionized the scientific study of living things. He was deeply committed to glorifying God through science. He called nature God's private garden. He believed that God was a God of order and creation followed this order.[14]

13. **Gregor Mendel (1822–1884)** was a Catholic priest, creationist, and scientist who is often called the "Father of Genetics." Famous for the study of reproduction and genetics, he was an Augustinian monk who studied how traits passed from parents to their offspring. Mendel showed that the inheritance of traits follows particular laws, which were later named after him. He gave up scientific pursuits in his later years. He believed that more emphasis should be put on spiritual matters than scientific things. He devoted a lot of his time and energy to fighting against governmental attacks against the religious liberties of the church.[15]

14. **Michael Faraday (1791–1867)** was an English chemist and physicist known as the "electrical giant." He discovered the laws of electrolysis, electromagnetic induction, hydroelectricity, the relationship between electricity and gravity, and atmospheric magnetism.[16] He made his Christian faith known and was not afraid to argue with any scientist who came against what he believed to be the truth about God and the reality of faith. He believed that nature substantiates the existence of its Creator. Because one God created the world, all of nature must be interconnected as a single whole.[17]

15. **James Clerk Maxwell (1831–1879)**, the founder of modern physics, created the mathematical equations that solidified the principles of physics. Maxwell's major aim in his research on electricity and magnetism was to produce the mathematical framework underlying Faraday's experimental results and his ideas on field theory. The four mathematical

equations Maxwell produced are ranked with Sir Isaac Newton's laws of motion and Albert Einstein's theory of relativity as the most fundamental contributions to physics.[18] He was a devout Christian and an example of what can be accomplished when science is approached from a biblical perspective. He was known for praying while performing scientific research.[19]

16. **James Joule (1818–1889)** was the founder of the First Law of Thermodynamics, the study of energy. Joule displayed an amazing clarity in conceiving, executing, describing, and explaining his experiments. Joule was a sincere Christian, known for his patience and humility. He believed in finding God's will and obeying it. It is recorded that he stated, "After the knowledge of and obedience to the will of God, the next aim must be to know something of His attributes of wisdom, power, and goodness as evidenced by His handiwork."[20]

The Bible says that the enemy comes to steal, kill, and destroy (John 10:10). After reading the accomplishments and testimonies of men of God who influenced scientific studies in such a great way, it is easy to see how the devil has attempted to steal precious information that counts. It is an honor for me to further the vision of these apostolic pioneers by writing this chapter. As we read our schoolbooks and wonder what happened to God in our society, it is no secret that the enemy has crept in unawares.

What was his strategy? During the era referred to as The Enlightenment, scientific study began to focus on the fact that the scientists of the past had made major mistakes. The new way of thinking was that scientific studies of the past had to be critically examined. All new studies had to be based on experiments and studies. As they stopped referring to the studies of past scientists, who were mostly Christian, they began to ignore the authority of the Bible. Slowly, references about God in science were hardly found. Eventually many professionals in this field of work began to question the authority of the Bible in science and even worked to prove that God did not exist.

The boldness of atheism escalated to an all-time high. Scientists like Charles Darwin, the founder of Darwinism, put an accepted way of thinking in place that explained man's existence totally excluding God. Darwin's ideas became popular with the powers that be in science. It empowered the antichrist agenda of those who denied God as the Creator. The theory of evolution reasoned that if science could explain how we began to exist without ever acknowledging a creator, why should science even assume that God even exists? Men chose to believe that we evolved from apes and became human beings rather than to believe that God created man and woman and they replenished and filled the earth.

As believers, we must teach our children the truth. Just as with Daniel and the Hebrew boys, God will give us voices and cause us to have divine favor in the midst of a corrupt system. The truth will make us free and liberate those who are bound by the deceptions of the devil.

We need pure science in America and around the world. My definition of *pure science* is: "science that makes God the foundation of all things." Any philosophies or thoughts that attempt to leave God out are impure ideologies that will one day be judged. Whoever takes on a title or a position of responsibility to teach outside of the realm of God as Creator and Jesus as Lord will ultimately fail and be eternally damned! There is no science without God.

As a matter of fact, anything learned about the world and why things are the way they are can only be found through the science of God. As we study God, we can find out about His creation and how He made things to be. Getting this revelation would settle the dispute over the land in Israel, stop abortions, protect the sanctity of marriage, and prevent people from becoming confused about their sexuality. Learning about God and how He made things to be *settles all matters!* The science of God is that He made all things. Any way that seems right in the minds of men but does not line up with God *will lead to death!*

CHAPTER 14

THOU SHALT NOT COVET

W E MUST PRACTICE spiritual economics to endure famines. I define *spiritual economics* as the method by which believers use biblical principles that relate to their provisions and prosperity to establish how they deal with their needs and wants. For the purpose of this chapter, I must define the words *needs* and *wants*.

1. *Needs*—a condition or situation in which something is required and cannot be done without

2. *Wants*—a condition or situation whereby something is wished for or desired but is not necessary

The Bible teaches that the children of Israel left Egypt (their place of bondage) with many material things. God caused the Egyptians to give the Israelites riches as they left the land. This was an awesome supernatural increase to a people who had been slaves for four hundred years (Gen. 15:13). The wealth of the wicked was transferred to the just. In the midst of their transition, while traveling through the wilderness, the people of God had needs that the Egyptians could not provide for them. For these needs they had to believe God. When they were hungry, God gave them manna. The manna was what they needed, but somehow their flesh wanted more. God gave them manna, but they coveted meat. God allowed them to have the meat, but He caused it to come out of their nostrils (Num. 11:20).

Coveting creates two states of the mind:

1. People who spend their lives lusting after what they can never have

2. People who have so much of what they wanted that their lives are miserable with it, and they have no rest

One of the most popular reality shows today is about rich housewives. The reality of their shows proves that it does not prosper a man to gain the whole world and lose his or her soul. Most of the women on these shows (not necessarily all of them) have plenty in the material realm, but they have no rest.

In Exodus 20:17, God told His people, "Thou shall not covet" (KJV). *Covet* is a key word in dealing with spiritual economics. It is defined as, "having an evil lust or desire for *things*." The greatest example of coveting that I have witnessed in my lifetime occurred this past Thanksgiving on Black Friday. A mob of shoppers trampled a Walmart worker to death. The doors were opened to shoppers in the wee hours of the morning, and the crowd lost it. They were so controlled by the *want* for things that they did not notice the smothering man trampled under their feet.

From a biblical standpoint, coveting falls under two main categories: people covet what belongs to someone else, or people covet what God has not given to them. To avoid these two evil conditions, we must understand the principles of *portion, lot,* and *inheritance.* A declaration we use in our church says, "What God has for me *is for me!*"

Those words confirm the revelation of *portion, lot,* and *inheritance.*

1. *Portion*—"My flesh and my heart fail; but God is the strength of my heart and my *portion* forever" (Ps. 73:26, emphasis added).

2. *Lot*—"O LORD, You are the portion of my inheritance and my cup; You maintain my *lot.* The lines have fallen to me in pleasant places; yes, I have a good inheritance" (Ps. 16:5–6, emphasis added).

3. *Inheritance*—"I love them that love me; and those that seek me early shall find me. Riches and honour are with me; yea, durable riches and righteousness. My fruit is better than gold, yea, than fine gold; and my revenue than choice silver. I lead in the way of righteousness, in the midst of the paths of judgment: That I may cause those that love me to inherit substance; and I will fill their treasures" (Prov. 8:17–21, KJV).

Study the definitions of the Hebrew words listed below:

1. *Portion (cheleq)*—"As smooth stones, used for a lot or that which has been set aside for distribution; separated unto a particular person"

2. *Lot (gowral)*—"A portion or destiny that is assigned by a lot that has determined it"

3. *Durable (`atheq)*—"Generational and of great value"

4. *Substance (yesh)*—"To exist; comes from the Hebrew word *yaresh,* which means to possess"

Based on these scriptures and word studies, I feel safe in making this comment:

> God has a portion for every life. This portion specifically falls upon individuals when they are in place and love God. Those who love God have a good heritage. As believers, we should seek God early and His kingdom first. As a result, we will receive durable riches that have been stored up for us through the generations and are of great value. What God has for His people is more valuable than the most precious things of the world. As we are led by God, it will be revealed that these riches actually exist and can be possessed.

Coveting is the enemy of the portion of the believer. We cannot be identified with unbelievers when it comes to provision. The Gospel of Matthew confirms this:

> Therefore do not worry, saying, "What shall we eat?" or "What shall we drink?" or "What shall we wear?" For after all these things the Gentiles [heathens] seek. For your heavenly Father knows that you need all these things. But seek first the kingdom of God and His righteousness, and all these things shall be added to you. Therefore do not worry about tomorrow, for tomorrow will worry about its own things. Sufficient for the day is its own trouble.
>
> —MATTHEW 6:31–34

The words "Thou shall not covet" is the medicine we need in the hearts of Americans to deal with the attacks against our economy. This revelation must start in the church. Keeping up with the Joneses is soon to be a thing of the past. We have found out that the Joneses could not keep up with their own lifestyle. The neighborhood that I live in is full of empty houses as a result of people who were living beyond their means. This is what coveting does—it deceives people into a false prosperity. False prosperity can be controlled by worldly economic situations. The prosperity of the Lord is forever and not subject to shifts in the economy. Women of warfare do not have to be afraid of spiritual winters because what God has for us... *it is for us!*

The Lord gave me a prophetic word on June 17, 2008. He said He would unbuckle the riches of the financially and intellectually strapped. He said that their understanding would become their enemy. As 1 Corinthians 1:19 declares, God has baffled the minds of the logicians, statisticians, and those who consider themselves learned concerning today's economy. They do not have a revelation of the bottomless pit of greed and lust, which has built a stronghold in our country. Greed, lust, and spirits that have caused men to covet are demonic forces that operate subliminally. They are the scales that cover the strongman of mammon. *Mammon*, in the Greek, means, "money personified." Riches and material things can take on personalities and become more real to people than God. It is idolatry! Coveting is a result of never having enough and opens the door to idolatry. This is why one of the characteristics of the personality of God is *more than enough.* He is *Jehovah-Jireh*—the Lord who sees and provides ahead of time.

In Joshua 7:21, Achan was a victim of the *spirit of coveting.* The Word of the Lord reads:

> When I saw among the spoils a beautiful Babylonian garment, two hundred shekels of silver, and a wedge of gold weighing fifty shekels, *I coveted them* and took them. And there they are, hidden in the earth in the midst of my tent, with the silver under it.
>
> —EMPHASIS ADDED

The desire to have these items came through Achan's eye gates. He saw them and had to have them. We have to be very careful of what we give constant attention to. Ladies, be careful what you watch on television and hold in high esteem. Our generation covets the wealth of people like Oprah, the fame of people like President

Obama, and the lifestyle of the rich and the famous. If the truth is really told, all of these things—without Jesus—are vortexes that pull people away from God into states of misery. Just as we monitor what our children are watching on television, we must also reinforce the fact that present fame and worldly glory are delusions. We must paint pictures of the depression, misery, and hopelessness that go on after the bright lights are turned off. Day only lasts a matter of short hours; eventually the night comes! Many can smile and pretend in the day, but when the night comes, the reality of life really manifests itself in the heart of a man. This is why we need God's light to shine in our hearts. When the night comes (and it will), the light from our hearts will show us the way. Many are lost in the darkness of depression and despair because the world has no light. We are the light of the world, and we cannot allow the spirit of lust to put our lamps out. The Bible says that the light of the virtuous woman always shines—it never goes out (Prov. 31:18). Being the virtuous woman that you are, you must continue to confess: "This little light of mine, I'm gonna let it shine!"

BEWARE OF THE SPIRIT OF ACHAN

Although God wants us to have nice things, we must keep our eyes on Jesus. Whatever we keep our eyes on—will *keep us!* Keeping our eyes on Jesus keeps us and protects us from lustful desires. On the other hand, if we keep our eyes on the wrong thing, *it will keep us in bondage!*

Achan took his eyes off the commandment of God and put them on things. This is the danger being released to this generation. The things of this world have the attention of the people more than the things of God.

A spirit has been released in America whereby people want something for nothing. They want get-rich-quick schemes and seek after overnight success. According to the principles of God, people who do not work should not eat (2 Thess. 3:10). As God shows in the parable of the talents, He will take from the people who do not have and give it to the ones who do have. (See Matthew 25:14–30.) This principle of how God deals with the haves and have-nots has nothing to do with the poor versus the rich. It refers to stewardship. The business owner in the parable of the talents gave talents to three men. He gave one talent to one man, two talents to one man, and five talents to another man. The men with two and five talents invested their talents and had something to show for it when the businessman returned. The man with one talent hid it in the ground and made excuses for what he did not have.

The message of this parable is not about how much a man has; on the contrary, it is about what a man does with what he has. The worst thing we can do with what God has given us is to lack appreciation. Bad stewardship manifests as a result of a lack of appreciation. The spirit of appreciation makes a person want to do something with what he or she has. As women of warfare, we must be good stewards of what God gives us. The first step of stewardship is appreciation.

The definition of the word *appreciate* is: "something recognized as being of worth, importance, or value; it also means to gain value."

It is easy to covet things when we overlook what we have and lack appreciation for it. Appreciation causes the value of a thing to increase. An example can be of a person who owns an old minivan but desires to purchase a Mercedes Benz 600-series. If this person is so consumed with getting the Mercedes that he neglects to appreciate the minivan, he can bring a curse upon himself. This curse is the curse of coveting, and it comes because of a lack of appreciation. There is nothing wrong with desiring better things. The sin comes in when a person depreciates the value of what he has by not being thankful. This is why the Bible says that we should be thankful in all situations and for all things. In Philippians 4:11 Paul stated that he knew to be content in "whatever state I am."

The steward of the one talent was so focused on what he did

not have that he could not see what he had. We must be able to consider and see what God has blessed us with from a thankful position. The business owner called the steward of the one talent wicked and good-for-nothing. "He who is slothful in his work is a brother to him who is a great destroyer" (Prov. 18:9). It is God's will that we work and be good stewards of the fruits of our labor.

What the Bible Says About Coveting

The Old Testament prophets touched on the sin of coveting. Habakkuk said:

> Woe to him who covets evil gain for his house,
> That he may set his nest on high,
> That he may be delivered from the power of disaster!
>
> —Habakkuk 2:9

Micah said:

> They covet fields and take them by violence,
> Also houses, and seize them.
> So they oppress a man and his house,
> A man and his inheritance.
>
> —Micah 2:2

Both prophets warn against coveting, but the words that we need to pay attention to are in Micah 2:2:

- *Fields (sadeh)*—Country, land, or place of birthright

- *House (bayith)*—Family

- *Heritage (nachalah)*—Portion, possession, inheritance or what has been rightfully handed down as if through an estate

Micah speaks of a territorial and generational spirit of covetousness that rules over families, countries, and even flows generationally through a man's heritage. Some people suffer from the manifestations of covetous spirits through these sources, and they must be dealt with through prayer and spiritual warfare. In dealing with territorial and generational spirits, they must be displaced. This means that the negative influence must be removed and replaced with a positive one. To displace the spirit of coveting, it must be replaced with contentment. Let's define *content*; it is simple and not deep—*to be happy with what you have!* It means to be satisfied or full.

Thanksgiving has recently passed as I am writing this chapter. I am sure that many people visited several homes of loved ones and family members. I had so much food that I was concerned that we could not store it all. Some of my family members had plates piled so high that I could not see their faces as I sat across from them. Just kidding! But they did eat a lot of food. If they had left my house to visit others, there is no way they could have eaten more. Even the best food in the world would have been turned down. Why? Because they were full! This is what being content means—to be full.

To make it through the economic situation we face today, we must be saved, sanctified, and satisfied. To be satisfied also means to have the issue settled in your heart to the point of not being needy. Being needy can easily lead to being greedy! God promises to supply all of our needs according to His riches in glory (Phil. 4:19). This was conditional and based upon the fact that in return the people supplied the needs of God's servant Paul. In general, the world cannot get this principle. They understand giving Caesar what belongs to him, but they mock giving God what belongs to Him. When we bless a man or woman of God, the seed does not stop at the human being. It goes straight to God! When we bless God's anointed, we bless Him! Paul understood this principle. He told the people that the reason they were being blessed was not because they gave according to his needs. He made it clear that his needs were met by the labor of his own hands.

OUR PROBLEM IN AMERICA

Coveting will definitely lead to debt. Many people were taken advantage of by the mortgage system in America. Some are in trouble because they coveted what another man had. Coveting comes against the promise of God that we will be lenders and not borrowers.

Before our economic crisis, I could not help but notice that many people were living extreme lifestyles in comparison to their incomes. I wondered how they had such large homes and fancy vehicles. In 2008, all my questions were answered and made clear to me. People were living *above* their means and had become slaves of debt. Paul warned the church in Rome, "Owe no man any thing, but to love one another" (Rom. 13:8, KJV)! Debt is the strongman that rules over the spirit of interest. Interest is a deep hole that you can never get out of. People need to get to the place where they are spiritually allergic to interest. It is a bondage that goes deeper than the natural. Many people have been living under the false prosperity of credit cards for years. As bad as the situation may seem, America has learned a valuable lesson—do not be a brother to the *great waster* (Prov. 18:9). Now we must humble ourselves, repent, and live within the means of our portion. It is the heritage of the just man. Do not attempt to keep up with wicked men in their worldly forms of prosperity.

> Arise, O Lord! Confront and forestall them, cast them down! Deliver my life from the wicked by Your sword, from men by Your hand, O Lord, from men of this world [these poor moths of the night] whose portion in life is idle and vain. Their bellies are filled with Your hidden treasure [what You have stored up]; their children are satiated, and

they leave the rest [of their] wealth to their babes. As for me, I will continue beholding Your face in righteousness (rightness, justice, and right standing with You); I shall be fully satisfied, when I awake [to find myself] beholding Your form [and having sweet communion with You].

—Psalm 17:13–15, amp

This is a prayer that David prayed to God. His prayer lines up with what his son Solomon later said about the wicked and their wealth. Remember, Solomon was a very rich man. He looked at all the work of his hands and noted that without God it was all vanity and vexation of the spirit. He made it clear that he thought that a man who loved silver, abundance, and increase would never be satisfied (Eccles. 5:10). In other words, if a man loves riches, he cannot help but covet, because he is never satisfied!

This is why Paul said that a man should love his neighbor as he loves himself (Rom. 13:9). In order to covet, you have to want something from a neighbor (or another person). In Romans 13:9, Paul teaches that when we love our neighbor, it sums up all the commandments such as thou shall not kill, steal, or commit adultery. This does not mean that it takes away from the fact that we should not commit these sins. It literally means that we fulfill these commandments by loving our neighbor, because if we love our neighbor, we would not commit these sins against him or her. It is hard to kill someone, steal from someone, or commit adultery without a *neighbor* (another person) being involved when you love that person as Christ called you to love him or her. When we love our neighbors as Christ called us to do, the purpose for God's commandments are manifested in the earth realm.

We can live prosperous lives by displacing ungodly covetousness with godly covetousness. It is scriptural. First Corinthians 12:27–31 teaches that we should covet the best gifts with a sincere heart. First Corinthians 14:39 says that we should covet to prophesy. Whenever deliverance takes place, the spot that was filled with the wrong things has to be refilled with the right thing. Once a person is delivered from covetousness, they must be filled with contentment.

In 1 Timothy, Paul had severe words for teachers of false doctrine who were puffed up in pride:

> And protracted wrangling and wearing discussion and perpetual friction among men who are corrupted in mind and bereft of the truth, who imagine that godliness or righteousness is a source of profit [a moneymaking business, a means of livelihood]. From such withdraw. [And it is, indeed, a source of immense profit, for] godliness accompanied with contentment (that contentment which is a sense of inward sufficiency) is great and abundant gain. For we brought nothing into the world, and obviously we cannot take anything out of the world; but if we have food and clothing, with these we shall be content (satisfied). But those who crave to be rich fall into temptation and a snare and into many foolish (useless, godless) and hurtful desires that plunge men into ruin and destruction and miserable perishing. For the love of money is a root of all evils; it is through this craving that some have been led astray and have wandered from the faith and pierced themselves through with many acute [mental] pangs. But as for you, O man of God, flee from all these things; aim at and pursue righteousness (right standing with God and true goodness), godliness (which is the loving fear of God and being Christlike), faith, love, steadfastness (patience), and gentleness of heart.
>
> —1 Timothy 6:5–11, AMP

True godliness is accompanied with contentment. This is the only true gain! Paul continued to discuss the issue with Timothy in the same chapter:

> As for the rich in this world, charge them not to be proud and arrogant and contemptuous of others, nor to set their hopes on uncertain riches, but on God, Who richly and

ceaselessly provides us with everything for [our] enjoyment. [Charge them] to do good, to be rich in good works, to be liberal and generous of heart, ready to share [with others], in this way laying up for themselves [the riches that endure forever as] a good foundation for the future, so that they may grasp that which is life indeed.

—1 TIMOTHY 6:17–19, AMP

Paul charged Timothy to challenge the rich. He told Timothy to warn them about pride. He also said to tell them to be careful not to set their hopes on "uncertain riches" for their future. Many people who are considered well off can learn a lesson from what Paul taught Timothy. They put their hopes in their 401K plans and other uncertain riches, but most of them still do not know that God is the one who ceaselessly provides. He provides whether the economy is doing well or not. This is why investing in the economy of God cannot be beat. Until this year I have never made any kind of investment. I have planted seeds in the good ground of the kingdom. While this year has been the worst for most, it has been the best year of my life financially. With God's help, I have been able to meet—and exceed—all the financial obligations of my ministry and of our personal lives. During times of economic turmoil in our nation, God supernaturally met our needs and paid off all of our debt. Many of these blessings were a confirmation to me of a prophetic word He gave me on June 17, 2008. I am not afraid of the snow for my house, and my household members are clothed in scarlet (Prov. 31:21).

COVET VS. CONTENT

This section is a comparative word study of the words *covet* and *content*. I pray the understanding of these terms can help you in your study time, prayer time, or to deliver a word from the Lord.

Scripture Reference	Greek or Hebrew Word	Definition
Covet		
Exodus 20:17	*chamad* (Strong's #2530)	"A desire to lust"
Romans 7:7; 13:9	*epithymeo* (Strong's #1937)	"To fain after, or give one's life for"
1 Corinthians 14:39; 12:31	*zeloo* (Strong's #2206)	"A zealous desire with jealousy and envy"
Content		
Genesis 37:27	*shama'* (Strong's #8085)	"Satisfaction that breeds obedience and gives attention; relates to discernment and having an ear to hear"
Exodus 2:21	*ya'al* (Strong's #2974)	"Contentment that causes mental weakness; that makes one yield and be willing"
1 Timothy 6:8	*arkeo* (Strong's #714)	"Sufficient; to have enough and be satisfied"
Philippians 4:11	*autarkes* (Strong's #842)	"To be self-complacent; pleased with one's self; untroubled; self-satisfied; not comparing one's self to others; not selfish but settled with the portion in life God has given"

The terms listed above put the icing on the cake in this chapter. It is clear that when we covet, we walk in a curse. It is an ungodly desire that leads to lust and causes a person to put God on the back burner. On the other hand, contentment is next to godliness. Paul wrote most of the New Testament and was famous for preaching the gospel. With all of the trials, tribulation, and persecution that came along with it, he was nevertheless *content*. He understood how *to do with* and how *to do without*.

Based on the meanings of the word *content* listed in the Bible, I can conclude that true contentment is:

> Satisfaction that sharpens the discernment of believers to have an ear to hear God. This satisfaction causes a mental weakness that forces a person to yield to God. Because this person is willing and obedient, he or she can eat of the good of the land and be full (satisfied). The end result of all that has taken place in this state of complacency is that the person walks in the blessing of *autarkes*. This is an inward self-satisfaction that cannot be affected or influenced by anything that happens in the environment—not even the present state of the economy. Selah.

The reason I feel that I am so prosperous is because it does not take much to please me. I am full of the blessings of God! Many people are more prosperous than the enemy allows them to see. Michael Jackson had so much success that he had an empty hole in his soul. People only saw the false success and could not discern the darkness that was really going on in his life. God bless his soul, but what could have been done to give him rest? He had everything in life, but all he wanted was rest. May his soul rest in peace; I cannot say where he is in eternity, for sure. I can say that he understands now that true contentment is only in Jesus Christ...wherever he is!

ROACHES IN A MANSION

> The desire of the slothful kills him, for his hands refuse to labor. He covets greedily all the day long, but the [uncompromisingly] righteous gives and does not withhold.
> —PROVERBS 21:25–26, AMP

Slothfulness, greed, and coveting walk hand in hand. There is nothing like lazy people in a house. I know that this is not a scripture, but it is a wise saying: "Cleanliness is next to godliness!" I always say: "There are demons in the dirt!" I cannot imagine living in a filthy house.

I once rented a house from a lady that looked immaculate. It was huge, in a gated community, and looked like a dream come true. After I moved in, I saw something move across the floor. It was my worst nightmare; the house had roaches! I thought, "How could anyone have a mansion filled with roaches?" They were not water bugs that flew inside when the door was opened; they were watermelon-seed-size roaches that only come from nastiness and filth. The real problem was that the owner of the house seemed to think this was not a serious issue.

To make a long story short, I debugged the house but learned a great lesson. Everyone does not appreciate the blessings of God. This house had six bedrooms and six bathrooms and looked pleasing to the eye. But if you spent enough time in it, you would easily see that not only did the house have roaches, but also it had not been given the attention it needed. I cannot say for sure why this house had problems. I can say that if we are lazy, things will go undone, and our standard of living will decline. If we are stingy and greedy and do not spend the money required to maintain things, it will cost us more in the long run. This lady did not even take the time to get a termite bond on a house worth over a million dollars.

What is the point of my telling this story? *Do not allow your spiritual mansion to have roaches!* Note that I am saying this from a spiritual perspective. Whatever God has given you *is your mansion*—take good care of it! Stewardship means everything in financial prosperity.

Slothfulness and Laziness

I have personally witnessed the spirit of laziness in the world of drug dealing. Because people are too lazy to get honest jobs, educations, or careers, they settle for evil gain. Proverbs 31:11 (AMP) says that because the husband of a virtuous woman believes in her, and can trust her and rely on her, he "has no lack of [honest] gain or need of [dishonest] spoil." In other words, the husband of a virtuous woman would not be comfortable dealing drugs or participating in illegal activities for gain.

The root of evil gain is coveting and never getting enough. The spirits of slothfulness, greed, and always wanting more tie a noose around the neck of their victims, and they are eventually hung. When I am ministering to people who I believe are selling drugs, I let them know that no matter how long they appear to succeed, it will be temporary. Eventually they will be killed in a conflict, forced to kill someone else, or locked up behind bars for the rest of their lives. The end of sin is death, and it never leads to a way out. It always leads to a physical or spiritual prison of bondage.

When we work and are good stewards of the work of our labor, we can enjoy it as God planned. As I read the Book of Ecclesiastes, I sensed the heart of one of the richest men who ever existed, King Solomon. The following scriptures stood out to me:

> So I saw that there was nothing better than that a man should rejoice in his own works, for that is his portion. For who shall bring him back to see what will happen after he is gone.
>
> —ECCLESIASTES 3:22, AMP

> Behold, what I have seen to be good and fitting is for one to eat and drink, and to find enjoyment in all the labor in which he labors under the sun all the days which God gives him—for this is his [allotted] part. Also, every man to whom God has given riches and possessions, and the power to enjoy them and to accept his appointed lot and to rejoice in his toil—this is the gift of God [to him]. For he shall not much remember [seriously] the days of his life, because God [Himself] answers and corresponds to the joy of his heart [the tranquility of God is mirrored in him].
>
> —ECCLESIASTES 5:18–20, AMP

Solomon bottom-lined it—the gift of God is to be able to enjoy and appreciate what God has given you in life! Solomon made it clear throughout the entire Book of Ecclesiastes that riches without God were vain and futile. He said that the only way a man can enjoy what God has given him is for God to keep him busy for joy and tranquility in his heart (Eccles. 5:20). This joy can be attained only through the peace of God. There is no peace in covetousness. I have learned that my portion is my blessing, and any more than that will make me miserable. Many ministers have so much more than I have materially. I rejoice in the prosperity of my brothers and sisters, but my joy is in the fact that I have what God has allotted for me. This is my contentment, and I never have to be under the curse of *almost* or *not enough*. I am full of my portion and have no room for what belongs to someone else.

Many people do not know how to recognize their portion because they do not have a relationship with the One who gave it. We must know God so that we can know what He has for us. What God has for me cannot be compared to another black, female, charismatic preacher. My blessing is tailor-made, and when God created it for me He broke the mold. It is all right to have role models; the problem starts when we try to walk in another man's portion or achieve his lot in life. Nobody can walk in my shoes because they were tailor-made for me. The confidence I have in this truth comes from knowing that if I attempt to walk in another man's shoes, I will trip and fall.

CHAPTER 15

THE BLESSINGS OF FIRSTFRUITS

THE FIRST WORD I ever heard from God was to seek Him first! Believers are called to seek the kingdom of God and His righteousness first, and everything that we need will be given unto us. We must put God first in our homes. As He blesses us, we must *bless Him*!

Proverbs 3:9 (AMP) commands us to honor the Lord: "with your capital and sufficiency [from righteous labors] and with the *firstfruits* of all our income (increase)" (emphasis added). When I came to God, He taught me about the principles of tithing. As I grew in the Lord, I understood that I had to go another level and become a *First Fruiter*. God blessed me through my tithing, and it kept the hand of the devourer off me. But when I began to understand and operate in the principle of firstfruits—I entered into my land! Let's read what the Bible says that we are supposed to do when we enter into our land.

When you have come into the land which the Lord your God gives you as an inheritance and possess it and live in it, you shall take some of the first of all the produce of the soil which you harvest from the land the Lord your God gives you and put it in a basket, and go to the place [the sanctuary] which the Lord your God has chosen as the abiding place for His Name [and His Presence]. And you shall go to the priest who is in office in those days, and say to him, I give thanks this day to the Lord your God that I have come to the land which the Lord swore to our fathers to give us. And the priest shall take the basket from your hand and set it down before the altar of the Lord your God. And you shall say before the Lord your God, A wandering and lost Aramean ready to perish was my father [Jacob], and he went down into Egypt and sojourned there, few in number, and he became there a nation, great, mighty, and numerous. And the Egyptians treated us very badly and afflicted us and laid upon us hard bondage. And when we cried to the Lord, the God of our fathers, the Lord heard our voice and looked on our affliction and our labor and our [cruel] oppression; and the Lord brought us forth out of Egypt with a mighty hand and with an outstretched arm, and with great (awesome) power and with signs and with wonders; and He brought us into this place and gave us this land, a land flowing with milk and honey. And now, behold, I bring the firstfruits of the ground which You, O Lord, have given me. And you shall set it down before the Lord your God and worship before the Lord your God.

—Deuteronomy 26:1–10, amp

The principles of firstfruits is more than a teaching; it is a mentality. When we put God first in our giving, our thought lives, our marriages and families, and our occupations and businesses, we will reap a greater harvest.

My family understands firstfruits to the point that we live a lifestyle of firstfruits. Everybody in the house knows that God comes first! I do not have to counsel my children about it or struggle with my husband over it.

Understanding firstfruits is not deep but is as simple as seeking and putting the things of God first. A firstfruit mentality comes from a first love. God does not want what we have left over; He wants our best—and He wants it before anything else. God wants to be our priority. In the Old Testament, when He blessed His people they acknowledged the fact that they knew where their blessings came from. They did this by giving God the best part of the first of their crop. This is called a *sheave offering*. The sheave was the first part of the blade that was seen sprouting from the ground. We have been having sheave offerings at the beginning of the year for five years in our church. Our ministry became debt free, and blessings have been running the people down and taking them over. I cannot begin to explain how honoring God with the first of my increase each year has blessed my house.

Because of this I created a word study with commentary so that the spirit of firstfruits can abide in your heart. This is not something that someone else can give you. You must get it for yourself. I pray that this word study will help you to *get it* so that the blessings of firstfruits can abide in your home.

This word study focuses on the following words:

- Firstfruits

- Increase

- Land

- Inheritance

- Possess

- Harvest

- Place

- Basket

The study includes English, Hebrew, and Greek definitions. In order to understand the essence of firstfruits, you must know the meaning of the words that pertain to it.

FIRSTFRUITS

The English definition is: "Giving God your best, or the choice part, from every area of your life." The key is *obedience*, seeking nothing in return, but the benefits will be bountiful.

Hebrew

- *Bikkuwr* (Strong's #1061)—refers to the yearly first gathering of the ripened produce of the land in honor of the fact that both the land and its produce belonged to the Lord. The produce was presented in a ceremony to the Lord in its harvested state. (See Exodus 23:16, 19.) This is called the day of firstfruits. On the Day of Pentecost, the people were actually gathering for the Feast of Firstfruits.

- *Re'shiyth* (Strong's #7225)—means beginning, first chief, best, most excellent, choicest part of the offering, best of the spoils, first of the harvest or firstborn of the father.

Greek

- *Aparché* (Strong's #536)—refers to the beginning of a sacrifice; firstfruits.

Commentary

The key word in dealing with the firstfruit offering is *honor*. To honor means, "to acknowledge and give the respect that is due." Often God's people have neglected to give Him the respect that is due unto Him concerning financial matters. Many people are not conscious of the fact that *everything* in the earth belongs to God, and He is gracious enough to allow us to steward over it.

The purpose of the firstfruit is to honor the Lord for the increase He has allowed us to experience. It is the highest level of thanksgiving unto the Lord. Because of this, it is important that the firstfruit offering is the best offering. In biblical history, livestock was offered to the Lord. It was considered a curse to not give God the choicest part of the harvest or the best of the spoils. There are accounts in the Bible where men offered God blemished livestock. This was not pleasing or even acceptable to the Lord. This was the case with Cain and Abel. A lukewarm mentality about Cain's offering is, "At least he gave something!" Well, this was not good enough for the Lord. The Lord explained to Cain that if he had done well, he would have been blessed (Gen. 4:7). This word *well* is *yatab*, and it means to please God.

Though we get blessed out of it, the main purpose of the firstfruit offering is to please God. It makes the statement from the heart of man to the heart of God: "Father, by giving You the first of my increase, I acknowledge that all I have belongs to You." It is important that firstfruit offerings are given from the heart.

The Bible states that God owns all the silver and the gold and the cattle on a thousand hills (Ps. 50:10). This is a fact, but it does not mean that men honor it. When we give firstfruit offerings to the Lord, it is an act of honor and obedience. It makes a statement (in the spirit) that Jesus is the Lord of the harvest in our lives and that we are obedient to the Word of God. The firstfruit is the beginning sacrifice of the year by which we give thanks for all that

God has done for the past year. I do not think that it is by chance that Pentecost took place on the day of firstfruits.

INCREASE

The English definition I would like to use for increase is: "growth that occurs as a result of multiplication that makes great."

Hebrew

- *Parats* (Strong's #6555)—to break out, break down and burst forth. This is a powerful multiplication that causes a spreading forth in all directions (especially the spreading of God's people so that they will be a blessing to all people according to the blessings of Abraham). This word refers to a birthing or a breaching of the womb and a demolition in the spirit that causes walls to fall down and crumble so that things held back can come.

- *Yacaph* (Strong's #3254)—To do again and cause continual increase that never ceases.

- *Yebuwl* (Strong's #2981)—refers to fruit or produce generated by a well-watered land. This word also represents increase brought forth by people who have labored.

- *Tebuw'ah* (Strong's #8393)—refers to revenue or income that has been produced from the ground. It notes prosperity as a benefit of wisdom (Prov. 3:14; 8:19). It also promotes the fact that all true increase comes from God.

- *Rabah* (Strong's #7235)—this definition depicts the increase of the Israelites in Egypt. It means to become numerous and great. It expresses God's original mandate for mankind to be fruitful and multiply in the earth, despite oppression and opposition.

- *Marbiyth* (Strong's #4768)—this word means profit or gain that comes from lending (Lev. 25:27). It also indicates the largest part or the extent or breadth of a thing. It is considered to be spiritually better off to be a lender than a borrower.

- *Shatham* (Strong's #8365)—this is increase that comes by the opening of the eyes. It brings revelation and opens the eyes for a person to receive. Many people are blinded by poverty, or they operate in less than what God calls them to operate in financially because they have scales on their eyes that need to be removed. Prosperity and increase cannot be received unless it can be seen. God promised Abraham that he could have His promises as far as he could see them.

Greek

- *Prostithemi* (Strong's #4369)—to annex, enlarge, or proceed further.

- *Auzano* (Strong's #837)—to grow up, enlarge, and give increase.

- *Pleonazo* (Strong's #4121)—to superabound and have more than what is needed.

- *Perisseuo* (Strong's #4052)—increase in quality and quantity that excels, makes better, and leaves enough to spare.

- *Prokopto* (Strong's #4298)—profit that causes advance that drives forth to wax great.

Commentary

The Hebrew and Greek words listed above prove that God wants His people to experience increase. Increase is not something we just read about in the Bible; it is reserved for the believer to partake of. Godly increase is not rooted in *having* but in *growing*. It is the process of God enlarging a person's coast, whereby they move from provision to superabundance over what is needed. This state takes the person from just *being blessed* into *becoming a blessing*, which causes gain that blesses others. I call it *being contagiously blessed*. The powerful multiplication of the blessings of God spreads in every direction and blesses those who come in contact with the blessed. Because they have come in contact with the blessing, these people are driven into *becoming* a blessing.

This is the power of the mustard seed spoken of in Matthew 13:31. It was the smallest seed God ever created and grew up to be a great tree. The birds that used to devour seeds the size of the mustard seed could then perch upon the branches of the tree. Godly increase causes a believer to be able to hold up what used to devour them. Street life used to devour me, but now because of the increase of God in my life, I can help a brother in the state that I used to be in. The power of godly increase is perfected when we use it to further the vision of the kingdom of God and to help others.

LAND

English definition: a nation—real or domain; the area of operation (AO) or coast that God has given; the domain of a person's dominion.

Hebrew

- *Yabbashah* (Strong's #3004)—land formerly covered with water, such as the land appearing on the third day of creation or the land on which the people crossed the Red Sea; also, land that water is poured onto (literally, and also as a figure of the Holy Spirit being poured on the descendants of Jacob, Isa. 44:3).

- *`Adamah* (Strong's #127)—means dirt, ground, or earth; signifies the substance of the ground from which God made Adam (the first man); Adam came from the ground and was also commanded to tend the ground; in a broader sense it means the inhabited earth (Gen. 4:2; Zech. 13:5).

- *`Erets* (Strong's #776)—refers to the whole earth under God's dominion; since the earth was God's possession, He promised to give Canaan to Abraham's descendants (Gen. 12:7; 15:7). The Promised Land is very important to Abraham's descendants (the nation of Israel); Israel's identity was tied to the land (Josh. 1:2, 4), because it signified the fulfillment of God's promise to Abraham. If the Israelites were disobedient, however, they would be cursed and would lose the land (Lev. 26:32, 34–38, 39; Deut. 28:63–64 [fulfilled in Dan. 3:6]; Jer. 7:7).

Greek

- *Ge* (Strong's #1093)—soil in distinction from a sea or lake; solid ground; the part of the earth that people can live in (upon the earth); that which can be tread upon; a region or country.

- *Xeros* (Strong's #3584)—dry; used of the body or its members; of the hand; a dry tree used to symbolize righteous and the wicked.

- *Chora* (Strong's #5561)—a field or place, district or territory; usually where cattle range and feed.

- *Agros* (Strong's #68)—cultivated ground; the country in distinction from cities or villages.

Commentary

The Promised Land represents coming into the promises of God. The Promised Land that Joshua invaded was not just natural, but spiritual. As he entered into the natural Promised Land called Canaan, so shall we as believers receive our inherited promise from God. There is a spiritual promised land or an area of operation (AO) for every believer. AO is a military acronym for place of assignment. Every promised land is connected to an assignment. When we get in the place of assignment, the place of the blessing is inevitable. We will inherit the land. Everything that God has promised us is connected to the land. When the people of God are in place, the earth must yield her increase! This is when the anointing will come from the soles of our feet and put a demand on the land to give it up. The land is already subdued—we must get in place to subdue it! All of humanity is called to walk in dominion in the earth realm. Because we are from the earth and called to tend it, the earth recognizes our authority.

When we get out of synchronization with God, the elements become confused. Man was made to walk with God! Our connection with dominion in the earth is directly connected with our relationship with God. When our relationship with God is severed, all of creation is put on hold and is out of synchronization. Creation then waits for the manifestation of the true sons of God. Creation has a revelation that man is made in God's image and called to dominion over it, even when men do not have a clue. In the meantime, men walk in false authority and power in the earth under the covering of the false one—Satan. This is how manifestations of false signs and wonders penetrate the earth realm and imitate the things of God. Only a close relationship with God can cause a person to have discernment to distinguish between the false and the genuine.

The devil can bless a person with things from the land. When Adam fell, Satan became the god of this world. The demonic supernatural was activated in the earth. This is why Abraham could not allow the king of Sodom to bless him. There are holy blessings and demonic blessings. Abraham gave the tenth of his increase to Melchizedek. We fall under that order today.

INHERITANCE

English definition: That which is received by genetic transmission; to receive from one's ancestors or one's lot in life; that which is given to a person through natural or spiritual lineage.

Hebrew

- *Nachal* (Strong's #5157)—(same definition for possess) to take property as a permanent possession; receiving land as: a gift from God (Exod. 23:30; 32:13); a tribal allotment (Josh. 16:4); a familial portion (Josh. 17:6). *Nachal* can also be used to describe acquiring other things than real property such as: a testimony (Ps. 119:111); glory (Prov. 3:35); good things (Prov. 28:10); simplicity (Prov. 14:18); blessings (Zech. 8:12).

- *Nachalah* (Strong's #5159)—property given by means of a will, a portion of an estate or blessing assigned by God; any possession presented by a father.

- *Mowrashah* (Strong's #4181)—this term refers to God's giving land to Israel; God's giving to other nations, and even to Israel's enemies (Ezek. 25:10). God also delivered the people of Israel over to other nations as a possession (Ezek. 25:4; 36:3). There were times when the people of Israel took high places as a possession (Ezek. 36:2).

Commentary

Your inheritance is a gift from God. It is a generational blessing. The curses go back four generations, but your blessings go forward for a thousand generations.

POSSESS

English definition: to have control of; to own property; to have knowledge or skill.

Hebrew

- *Yarash* (Strong's #3423)—to inherit by dispossession or driving out; sometimes refers to generational inheritance but mostly connected to the idea of conquering a land.

- *Nachal* (Strong's #5157)—see *inheritance*.

- *Chacan* (Strong's # 2631)—to hold in occupancy or occupy or possess the land; refers to the passing of the kingdom to the saints of the Most High, to their taking over its administration (Dan. 7:18, 22; Rom. 8:17; 1 Pet. 2:9; Rev. 3:21).

Commentary

Inheritance and possession walk hand in hand. The difference between the two is that the inheritance is more connected to coming from a father and what he hands down through his lineage. The inheritance of the Father is not limited to natural possessions. It includes good things, simplicity, blessings, and glory. It is a blessing to have peace of mind daily. This is a good thing. It is dangerous to focus on material good things as a priority. We should set our sights on things of the spirit first. This is the most important thing to remember about firstfruits—putting first things first!

There are demonic blessings and holy blessings. In Genesis 1:22, God blessed Adam and Eve. The Hebrew word for *blessed* is *barak*. As I studied this word, I discovered that this word included blessings and curses. The roads of the blessing and the curse are parallel in the spirit. Which is received depends on obedience to God according to Deuteronomy 28. The devil lies in wait to seduce anyone who tries to get the blessing without being obedient to God. He is authorized to manifest a false blessing, because he is the god of this world. He is the angel of light.

The biggest secret in the church is that the devil can bless people. To discern between the demonic blessing and the holy blessing is not hard but simple. Those who plunge too deeply will miss what I am saying, because the blessings of the Lord are clothed in simplicity. Blessings that come from the demonic realm are complicated. The blessings of the Lord make you light and bring rest. Blessings from the dark side frustrate and weigh heavily on the mind. The blessings of the Lord put pressure on the soul to fall into a deeper relationship with God, but the demonic blessings root the heart of a man to love money more! The blessings of the Lord are true wealth, but the blessings of the devil are manifestations of the god called *Mammon*. *Mammonas* is money personified or money that becomes more real in the minds of men than God. *Mammonas* is the god of materialism and the love of all kinds of possessions, earnings, and gains. It releases a spirit in the land whereby men have to have things by any means necessary. It is a deception, because if man puts God first according to Matthew

6, he will get things automatically. You do not have to sell your soul to get things. I have often marveled when people tried to step on me or come against me to get things. I just kept my eyes on the kingdom, and God gave me the things they were fighting for. When Matthew 6 tells us to seek the things of the kingdom first, God meant just that. The word *first* is *proton*. It means, "first in order or priority." God is calling us to be proton believers. My mentor/apostle, John Eckhardt, has a book called *Proton Believers*. When we put God first, we always come out on top.

God has given His people the power to get wealth according to Deuteronomy 8. It is prophesied in Daniel 7:22 that the time will come for the saints to possess the kingdom. Only the proton believers will do so. This is our ultimate inheritance. It is off limits to the wicked because it is reserved for the just.

Harvest

English definition: the season for gathering mature crops that bring great increase.

Hebrew

- *Qatsiyr* (Strong's #7105)—implicates a reaping of what has been sown; it refers to a time of the year (set by God) for crops to ripen for gathering; a fresh springing forth that indicates new life.

Greek

- *Therismos* (Strong's #2326)—this term refers to the harvesting of souls that are ripe for the kingdom versus those whose iniquity is fully ripe for punishment. The harvest of *therismos* is a separating of the wheat from the tares.

Commentary

In biblical times, having no harvest was considered wicked. The signature of the righteous was the harvest of the Lord. God blessed His people with divine provision despite times of famine to confirm His covenant with them. A cut-off or dead branch is biblically evil because it can bring no harvest. The people of God are blessed because they are healthy branches connected to the source (Jesus Christ). Jesus declares that He is the vine, and we are the branches. A branch cannot have a harvest of itself except it abide in the vine. Abiding in the vine is not a choice; it is a commandment. Those who do not abide in the vine (Jesus) will be cut off and cast into the fire (John 15:4–6). Having a harvest is connected to the eternal lifeline of the believer. In Christ, there is no failure of harvest. Harvest is not bound by economic categories, groups, or the interpretation of men. True harvest brings manifold blessings that break out from the vine and flow in every direction. Those connected to the vine will receive manifold more. This blessing does not come without a price. The manifold more is undergirded in sacrifices made for the kingdom.

When Jesus explained the parable of the rich young ruler to the disciples, He said:

> For it is easier for a camel to go through the eye of a needle than for a rich man to enter the kingdom of God.
>
> —LUKE 18:25

He told the rich young ruler:

> You still lack one thing. Sell all that you have and distribute to the poor, and you will have treasure in heaven; and come, follow Me.
>
> —LUKE 18:22

The young man wanted to know what he could do to inherit the kingdom of God. Jesus was only saying to him, "Son, to follow Me, you must cut all of your soul ties (things that keep your soul out of the kingdom)." It was apparent the young man loved his stuff more than God. He did not consider Jesus's words. He walked away sad because mammon had a grip on his soul. Serving Jesus is a sacrifice! Sadly, many walk away from God because they love people, places, and things more.

Peter responded to Jesus by saying, "Lord, we have left everything to follow you!"

Jesus then said:

> Assuredly, I say to you, there is no one who has left house or parents or brothers or wife or children, for the sake of the kingdom of God, who shall not receive many times more in this present time, and in the age to come eternal life.
>
> —Luke 18:29–30

Place

English definition: space, room region, position, locality, or purpose.

Hebrew

- *Maqowm* (Strong's #4725)—Deuteronomy 26:2 refers to the place that God chooses; chosen place or a designated place that is holy because it is separated unto God.

- *Shakan* (Strong's #7931)— Deuteronomy 26:2 refers to the place for God's name; it means to settle down, rest, and dwell; God established this place by setting up a dwelling place for His name to abide.

Commentary

When Jehoshaphat got out of place with God, the prophet prophesied that he had to go to the Ascent of Ziz (2 Chron. 20:16). Though this was a physical locality, it has a spiritual connotation. There is a place in the spirit that we must go to receive the blessings of God. I call it the place called *THERE*. In Deuteronomy 26, God did not only focus on the gift of the firstfruit; the person had to be in place to give it. Each person had to pay attention to the details that God gave as to how He wanted the firstfruit presented. It had to be:

- Given in the place that God chose

- A place where God's name rested

- A place that God had brought His people (they had to spiritually be in place)

Basket

English definition: a receptacle made of interwoven material.

Hebrew

- *Cal* (Strong's #5536)—refers to a container with the ability to hold something.

- *Duwd* (Strong's #1731)—refers to baskets of bondage that the Israelites were forced to carry by the Egyptians. In Jeremiah 24:2, Jeremiah had a vision of a basket of figs.

- *Kelub* (Strong's #3619)—a basket specifically made to carry fruit. In Amos 8:1, it was seen in a prophetic vision. This fruit was ripe and about to perish. God said that He would not pass by the iniquities of His people and continue to spare them. He said the songs of the temple would become wailing.

- *Tene'* (Strong's #2935)—a container used for the offering from the ground of the Promised Land of Canaan; used to symbolically represent the rich abundance of the ground.

Greek

- *Spuris* (Strong's #4711)—a basket for storing provision.

Commentary

In Deuteronomy 2, the basket referred to was the one that could contain the offering from the ground. Haggai warned of a curse that would cause increase to slip through like a hole in a bag (Hag. 1:6). It is no secret that believers must have spiritually strong containers to hold the increase that God gives His people. A python spirit is witchcraft released against finances that causes more to go out than comes in. Prosperity is simple. It is not how much you have, but the balance of how much goes out and how much comes in. When you have more coming in than the amount that is going out, it is increase or profit. Having a foundation of this principle will lead to even more profit. God wants to bless our baskets until there is no more room to receive. This is the overflow! This is what is being contagiously blessed—having so much overflow that you cannot help but bless the people around you. The only thing that could hinder this process is a greedy, hoarding spirit. When God gives more than enough, He wants our abundance to be our testimony that runs over into the lives of others.

A basket is also representative of that which stores for a later need.

> And if you say, "What shall we eat in the seventh year, since we shall not sow nor gather in our produce?" Then I will command My blessing on you in the sixth year, and it

will bring forth produce enough for three years. And you shall sow in the eighth year, and eat old produce until the ninth year; until its produce comes in, you shall eat of the old harvest.

—LEVITICUS 25:20–22

This is a very important passage of Scripture in relation to the firstfruit. It must be applied to deal with the economic situation in America today. The firstfruit offering opens the door to the Command Blessing. I can relate the Command Blessing to how department stores operate every year during the holiday season. The money these stores make during the holidays sustains them until the next holiday season. If a store does not do well during the holidays, its success throughout the year following will be challenged. The money made during the holiday season—including the day after Thanksgiving—overflows into the next year's provision, creating a *basket of old store*. In the scripture above, the people asked God: "How can we survive during the seventh year when there is no increase?" God said that He would send a Command Blessing on the sixth year. He also said that He would send enough for three years.

IN CONCLUSION

The firstfruit offering releases a fresh anointing, and it must be given willingly. The word *willingly* is *nadab* in the Hebrew, and it means, "to give with natural inclination or impulse and not from external manipulation or excitement." Women have been the major financiers of the kingdom of God forever. How can I say this? We cannot deny that women are filling the chairs on Sunday morning. Even if their husbands are providers, wives most likely make sure the tithes and offerings are given. If there are more women in the church, there are more women giving. I believe that women generally spend more money than men. We are the real-deal shoppers!

Most of the time, husbands dread shopping. I know my husband does! While I am in the stores having the time of my life, he is usually sitting in the mall looking like he wished he were some place else. As for me, shopping is in my veins, and I never had a struggle spending money to get what I wanted. Until I met Jesus, shopping was my first love. Even when I had only a little money, I always set something aside to buy something new every so often. If I could take back the money that I have spent in stores in my past and give it to God, the offering would be great.

When I purchased things while I was shopping, I never felt badly about it. As a matter of fact, shopping made me feel better. Even if I did not have that much money left when I got home, I did not regret what I had spent. Actually, I usually showed off what I had bought to my husband or kids. Why is it so easy for the enemy to hinder us from giving God our best? The enemy wants to make us sad givers, when God has called us to be cheerful givers. I want God to see that I enjoy giving to Him more than I enjoyed shopping at the mall. I want the Lord to see that I feel good about my giving, even when I have to sacrifice something else to do it.

As proud as I was about my purchase from the mall, today I take pride in giving God my best. This is what firstfruit offerings are all about—giving God the first or best that I have, mentally, spiritually, and financially. I found out that when I gave God the firstfruit of my material and financial increase, order was set in place to give Him the first in every area of my life. God wants the first of our time, to be first in the order of our relationships, the first of our thought life, and the first of even our motives in our calling. God will not take the back seat in any area of our lives. The greatest victory we can achieve as women of warfare is to learn to put God first. Putting God first opens the doors to the benefits of *nadab* in our lives. The liberty of giving freely from the heart, without struggle, is a blessing from God. The reciprocal benefits of this blessing are unimaginable. You see, when a person is liberated in giving, that person is released into new realms of financial prosperity.

Unconstrained, unstudied, Spirit-led giving without pressure causes a new river of financial freedom. A person who gives under pressure may as well keep the money in his or her pocket. Pressure takes the joy out of giving, and God loves a cheerful giver. This does not mean that a person should have to pump himself or herself up at every offering. It means that we should live lifestyles of cheerfulness that create giving hearts. Giving hearts create giving atmospheres. This is the best offering we can give God. The attitudes and atmospheres from which we give mean everything to God.

In Amos 4:4–5 the people gave thanksgiving offerings in great distress and not out of thankful hearts. They were offering to try to gain God's favor, but God rejected them because they were not given with the right attitude of thanksgiving and atmosphere of love. *Salem* is the Hebrew word for the thanksgiving offering. It is also called the *peace offering*. It gives true thanks and praise to God.

Firstfruit offerings must:

1. Be offered willingly

2. Make the people rejoice

3. Be given from a perfect heart

I know that no one is perfect, but the term *perfect heart* is related to the Hebrew word *salem*. It means to have a heart that is full, satisfied, complete, whole, and full of peace. If a firstfruit offering is not given from a peaceful heart, the purpose of the offering is taken away.

In the past, I have witnessed people who gave firstfruit offerings with the wrong attitudes and expectations. They did not have peace in their giving, and they did not reap the benefit of the offering. It is important that firstfruit offerings are given in faith with understanding. The firstfruit can be the first and the best offering of the year, a first income from a new job, the first increase from a new business, or the firstfruit of your time. This is why I believe that it is important to rise early and commune with God at the first of the daybreak. It establishes things before we go into our business of the day. Firstfruit are sacrifices, but the key word is *obedience*. Obedience is better than sacrifice. Though our congregation has a dedicated time for firstfruits as a ministry, every family should dedicate their first to God in obedience to how He would have them to do it.

All firstfruit offerings must be given by faith. On the other hand, understanding the principle of firstfruits must be put into effect. Faith without works is dead.

We cannot become firstfruit givers unless we pay our tithes first. The firstfruit is an offering, and it cannot be given until we pay God what we owe Him first. We owe tithes, and they are due to be paid. We give free-will offerings. This principle must be understood. A person once told me he only pays tithes *sometimes*. This is impossible. The word *tithe* means "tenth," and if we do not give a tenth of our income, we have not tithed. Since a debt is still owed to God, no offering can take place until the debt is paid in full.

I believe that the greatest warfare believers receive is in the area of giving. When we increase our giving, it will bring increase to our living. Jesus came that we might have abundant life. He has called our families to be healthy and prosperous. The devil does everything he can to steal, kill, and destroy our increase. He even uses ignorance about biblical principles, which affects our finances and kills our increase. By becoming firstfruit givers, we push him farther out of this area of our lives. When we put God first, the devil automatically becomes last and has no power. He is under our feet, and God rules over our heads.

I pray the blessings of the covenant of Abraham upon your

house. I decree that the favor of Obed Edom will rest over your roof and drip down under the foundation of your floor.

As for me and my house, we will serve the Lord—and we will serve Him, FIRST!

L AST BUT NOT least, I could not finish this book without dedi-cating a prayer to the children..."the seed of the home." If seed is not nurtured, it will never mature into what it is called to be. There is no prosperity without posterity! My household is not blessed unless my seed is blessed. I pray for God to bless my chil-dren daily. I teach them to decree and declare the blessings and protection of the Lord for themselves. Below is a prayer that I wrote for my children to confess before they start each day. I personal-ized the prayer by calling it "My Daily Prayer" for my children. I pray that as your children read this prayer they will be strength-ened in the Lord to be all they are called to be. I also pray that as they grow in the Word of the Lord, their hearts will be filled with wisdom and they will live long prosperous lives.

My Daily Prayer

Father God, I worship and reverence You. You are Lord!
I declare that this is a day that You have made, and I will
rejoice and be glad in it. Nothing can steal my joy today,

because Your joy is my strength. I am Your child, and You are my God. I dedicate my day to You. As I participate in my daily activities I thank You ahead of time for providing all my needs and protecting me from all danger. I put on the whole armor of God and plead the blood of Jesus over my day. My mind is buckled down with the helmet of salvation and being renewed every day. I am in tune with Your Holy Spirit, and I will make godly decisions today. I will not be influenced by peer pressure, the pressure of my flesh, or the pressures of this world. I am a child of the King, an heir of God and a joint-heir with Christ. Every plan and trap of the enemy against me is bound and blocked. I am under an open heaven, and I bind every accident and incident that would rise up to interrupt the flow of the destiny of God for my life.

The favor of God is strong on my life. Every vehicle, plane, or any other mode of transportation that I take is covered by the blood of Jesus. No freak accidents, incidents, arrows by day, or terrors by night can affect me as I participate in my school, work, and sports activities. Lord, I thank You ahead of time for delivering me from robberies, car-jacking, terrorist attacks, kidnappings, sexual predators, sabotages, setups, demonic pranks, school fights, gang initiations, natural disasters, and anything the devil may plan for my day. My day is established in You. I am Your child, and the path for my day has been made safe and prosperous. My Destiny Angel has gone before me. Guardian angels will surround me throughout the day. They will escort me from the morning until I am safely in my bed tonight. As I close my eyes, I will have divine rest and sweet sleep with no interference from nightmares, witchcraft, and demonic activity. Thank You, Jesus. Amen.

—By Kimberly Daniels (for my children)

Firstfruit Scriptures

Read aloud and pray the scriptures on firstfruits listed below over your house.

Old Testament

> Also you shall keep the Feast of Harvest [Pentecost], [acknowledging] the firstfruits of your toil, of what you sow in the field. And [third] you shall keep the Feast of Ingathering [Booths or Tabernacles] at the end of the year, when you gather in the fruit of your labors from the field.
>
> —Exodus 23:16, AMP

> You shall observe the Feast of Weeks, the firstfruits of the wheat harvest, and the Feast of Ingathering at the year's end. Three times in the year shall all your males appear before the Lord God, the God of Israel. For I will cast out the nations before you and enlarge your borders; neither shall any man desire [and molest] your land when you go up to appear before the Lord your God three times in the year. You shall not offer the blood of My sacrifice with leaven; neither shall the sacrifice of the Feast of the Passover be left until morning. The first of the firstfruits of your ground you shall bring to the house of the Lord your God. You shall not boil a kid in his mother's milk.
>
> —Exodus 34:22–26, AMP

As an offering of firstfruits you may offer leaven and honey to the Lord, but they shall not be burned on the altar for a sweet odor [to the Lord, for their aid to fermentation is symbolic of corruption in the human heart].

—LEVITICUS 2:12, AMP

If you offer a cereal offering of your firstfruits to the Lord, you shall offer for it of your firstfruits grain in the ear parched with fire, bruised and crushed grain out of the fresh and fruitful ear.

—LEVITICUS 2:14, AMP

Tell the Israelites, When you have come into the land I give you and reap its harvest, you shall bring the sheaf of the firstfruits of your harvest to the priest.

—LEVITICUS 23:10, AMP

You shall bring from your dwellings two loaves of bread to be waved, made from two-tenths of an ephah of fine flour; they shall be baked with leaven, for firstfruits to the Lord.

—LEVITICUS 23:17, AMP

All the best of the oil, and all the best of the [fresh] wine and of the grain, the firstfruits of what they give to the Lord, to you have I given them.

—NUMBERS 18:12, AMP

Also in the day of the firstfruits, when you offer a cereal offering of new grain to the Lord at your Feast of Weeks, you shall have a holy [summoned] assembly; you shall do no servile work.

—NUMBERS 28:26, AMP

And now, behold, I bring the firstfruits of the ground which You, O Lord, have given me. And you shall set it down before the Lord your God and worship before the Lord your God.

—DEUTERONOMY 26:10, AMP

[At another time] a man from Baal-shalisha came and brought the man of God bread of the firstfruits, twenty loaves of barley, and fresh ears of grain [in the husk] in his sack. And Elisha said, Give to the men that they may eat.

—2 KINGS 4:42, AMP

As soon as the command went abroad, the Israelites gave in abundance the firstfruits of grain, vintage fruit, oil, honey, and of all the produce of the field; and they brought in abundantly the tithe of everything.

—2 CHRONICLES 31:5, AMP

And [we obligate ourselves] to bring the firstfruits of our ground and the first of all the fruit of all trees year by year to the house of the Lord.

—NEHEMIAH 10:35, AMP

And we shall bring the first and best of our coarse meal, our contributions, the fruit of all kinds of trees, of new wine, and of oil to the priests, to the chambers of the house of our God. And we shall bring the tithes from our ground to the Levites, for they, the Levites, collect the tithes in all our rural towns.

—NEHEMIAH 10:37, AMP

On that day men were appointed over the chambers for the stores, the contributions, the firstfruits, and the tithes, to gather into them the portions required by law for the priests and the Levites according to the fields of the towns, for Judah rejoiced over the priests and Levites who served [faithfully].

—NEHEMIAH 12:44, AMP

And I provided for the wood offering at appointed times, and for the firstfruits. O my God, [earnestly] remember me for good and imprint me [on Your heart]!

—NEHEMIAH 13:31, AMP

Honor the Lord with your capital and sufficiency [from righteous labors] and with the firstfruits of all your income.

—PROVERBS 3:9, AMP

Israel was holiness [something set apart from ordinary purposes, dedicated] to the Lord, the firstfruits of His harvest [of which no stranger was allowed to partake]; all who ate of it [injuring Israel] offended and became guilty; evil came upon them, says the Lord.

—JEREMIAH 2:3, AMP

For on My holy mountain, on the mountain height of Israel, says the Lord God, there all the house of Israel, all of them in the land, shall serve Me. There will I [graciously] accept them, and there will I require your offerings and the firstfruits and the choicest of your contributions, with all your sacred things.

—EZEKIEL 20:40, AMP

And the first of all the firstfruits of all kinds, and every offering of all kinds from all your offerings, shall belong to the priests. You shall also give to the priest the first of your coarse meal and bread dough, that a blessing may rest on your house.

—EZEKIEL 44:30, AMP

And they shall not sell any of it or exchange it; they shall not convey or transfer this the firstfruits of the land, for it has been offered to the Lord and is holy to Him.

—EZEKIEL 48:14, AMP

New Testament

And not only the creation, but we ourselves too, who have and enjoy the firstfruits of the [Holy] Spirit [a foretaste of the blissful things to come] groan inwardly as we wait for the redemption of our bodies [from sensuality and the grave, which will reveal] our adoption (our manifestation as God's sons).

—ROMANS 8:23, AMP

[Remember me] also to the church [that meets] in their house. Greet my beloved Epaenetus, who was a firstfruit (first convert) to Christ in Asia.

—ROMANS 16:5, AMP

But the fact is that Christ (the Messiah) has been raised from the dead, and He became the firstfruits of those who have fallen asleep [in death]. For since [it was] through a man that death [came into the world, it is] also through a Man that the resurrection of the dead [has come]. For just as [because of their union of nature] in Adam all people die, so also [by virtue of their union of nature] shall all in Christ be made alive. But each in his own rank and turn: Christ (the Messiah) [is] the firstfruits, then those who are Christ's [own will be resurrected] at His coming.

—1 CORINTHIANS 15:20–23, AMP

Now, brethren, you know that the household of Stephanas were the first converts and our firstfruits in Achaia (most of Greece), and how they have consecrated and devoted themselves to the service of the saints (God's people).

—1 CORINTHIANS 16:15, AMP

And it was of His own [free] will that He gave us birth [as sons] by [His] Word of Truth, so that we should be a kind of firstfruits of His creatures [a sample of what He created to be consecrated to Himself].

—JAMES 1:18, AMP

These are they who have not defiled themselves by relations with women, for they are [pure as] virgins. These are they who follow the Lamb wherever He goes. These are they who have been ransomed (purchased, redeemed) from among men as the firstfruits for God and the Lamb.

—REVELATION 14:4, AMP

Chapter 4
Get the Occult Out of Your House

1. For additional information about Nicolas of Antioch, see "Nicolas," *Forerunner Commentary*, BibleTools.org, http://www.bibletools.org/index.cfm/fuseaction/Topical.show/RTD/cgg/ID/1776/Nicolas.htm (accessed March 17, 2011).

Chapter 5
Stand for the Truth in Your Home

1. Alan Guttmacher Institute, "Facts on Induced Abortion in the United States," http://www.guttmacher.org/pubs/fb_induced_abortion.html (accessed March 17, 2011).

2. Associated Press, "Militia Accused of Plotting War on U.S. Gov't," March 30, 2010, FOXNews.com, http://www.foxnews.com/us/2010/03/28/arrests-alleged-militia-activity-midwest/ (accessed March 17, 2011).

3. HealthCare 2.0, "Title I—Protections and Standards for Qualified Health Benefits Plans," HR-3200 Uncut Version, Segment #1, http://healthcare2point0.com/HR3200_uncutVer_part1.htm (accessed March 17, 2011).

4. Stephanie Condon, "Va. Lawmakers Oppose Forced Microchip Implantation, and the Antichrist," *Political Hotsheet* (blog), February 10, 2010, http://www.cbsnews.com/8301-503544_162-6195506-503544.html (accessed March 17, 2011).

Chapter 9
Close the Vortexes of Hell to Your Family Bloodline

1. USGS.gov, "Largest and Deadliest Earthquakes by year, 1990–2010," http://earthquake.usgs.gov/earthquakes/eqarchives/year/byyear.php (accessed March 21, 2011).

Chapter 12
The Science of God

1. WordIQ.com, "Alchemy—Definition," http://www.wordiq.com/definition/Alchemy (accessed March 22, 2011).

Chapter 13
The Apostles of the Science of God

1. Britannica.com, "Western Philosophy: Robert Grosseteste and Roger Bacon," *Encyclopaedia Britannica*, http://www.britannica.com/EBchecked/topic/1350843/Western-philosophy/8648/The-age-of-the-Schoolmen?anchor=ref365749 (accessed March 23, 2011). For more information about Grossesteste, see: "Robert Grosseteste," *Catholic Encyclopedia*, http://www.newadvent.org/cathen/07037a.htm (accessed March 23, 2011).

2. Conservapedia.com, "Roger Bacon," http://www.conservapedia.com/Roger_Bacon (accessed March 23, 2011).

3. NewAdvent.org, "Thomas of Bradwardine," *Catholic Encyclopedia*, http://www.newadvent.org/cathen/14693b.htm (accessed March 23, 2011).

4. Stanford.edu, "Cusanus, Nicolaus [Nicolas of Cusa]," *Stanford*

Encyclopedia of Philosophy, http://plato.stanford.edu/entries/cusanus/ (accessed March 23, 2011).

5. ChristianHistory.net, "Nicholas Copernicus," http://www .christianitytoday.com/ch/131christians/scholarsandscientists/ copernicus.html?start=2 (accessed March 23, 2011).

6. Dan Graves, *Scientists of Faith* (Grand Rapids, MI: Kregel Resources, 1996), 49.

7. J. J. O'Connor and E. F. Robertson, "Galileo Galilei," http:// www-history.mcs.st-and.ac.uk/Biographies/Galileo.html (accessed March 23, 2011).

8. As quoted in Bill Bright, *Jesus and the Intellectual* (San Bernardino, CA: Campus Crusade for Christ International, 1968).

9. Carol Hodanbosi, "Pascal's Principle and Hydraulics," National Aeronautics and Space Administration, http://www.grc .nasa.gov/WWW/k-12/WindTunnel/Activities/Pascals_principle .html (accessed May 11, 2011).

10. Reformation.org, "Sir Isaac Newton, http://www .reformation.org/newton.html (accessed March 23, 2011).

11. Graves, *Scientists of Faith,* 63.

12. Graves, *Scientists of Faith,* 70–71.

13. Dietrich Heinrich Stoever, *The Life of Sir Charles Linnaeus,* trans. Joseph Trapp (London: B. and J. White, Fleet Street, 1794).

14. Graves, *Scientists of Faith,* 80–83.

15. Creationwiki.org, "Gregor Mendel," http://creationwiki.org/ Gregor_Mendel (accessed March 23, 2011).

16. "Michael Faraday," http://depts.washington.edu/chemcrs/ bulkdisk/chem152A_win08/notes_Faraday.pdf (accessed May 11, 2011).

17. Adherents.com, "The Religious Affiliation of the Great Physicist Michael Faraday," http://www.adherents.com/people/pf/ Michael_Faraday.html (accessed March 23, 2011).

18. Ann Lamont, "James Clerk Maxwell," AnswersinGenesis .org, http://www.answersingenesis.org/home/area/bios/jc_maxwell. asp (accessed March 23, 2011).

19. Graves, *Scientists of Faith*, 150–153.

20. J. G. Crowther and K. Paul Trency, *British Scientists of the 19th Century* (London: Trubner & Co. Ltd., 1935), 138.

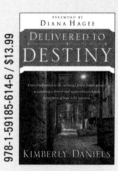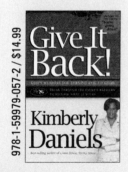